COLORED, OF COURSE

by

Shirley F. B. Carter

Goose River Press
Waldoboro, Maine

For order information please e mail the author at:
coloredofcourse@gmail.com

Cover by Kira Beaudoin.

ISBN: 978-1-59713-027-1

Library of Congress Control Number: 2006929077

Seventh Printing, 2012

Published by
Goose River Press
3400 Friendship Road
Waldoboro, Maine 04572
e mail: gooseriverpress@roadrunner.com
www.gooseriverpress.com

TABLE OF CONTENTS

TABLE OF CONTENTS

PART TWO: Learning about Life

PART THREE: Making My Way

TABLE OF CONTENTS

FOR MY DAUGHTERS
Laura & Mia

Acknowledgements

It is impossible to credit all the friends and contacts that merit mention and recognition. I must thank my family, especially my daughters: Mia and Laura to whom this book is dedicated and Audrey Brown, the sister with whom I was raised. Posthumous thanks go to a dear friend, Inés Eskenás de Rebecca and a very special creative writing professor, Robert L. Walker, who taught at Worcester State College. Each in their own way prompted me to share my story...that began as an essay describing my experiences of racism and its affect on my life.

Writing is a joy for me; the challenge and the appreciation come from my attempts to publish! There are at least sixty publishers and agents I can thank for answering my queries. My goal was to send and receive at least one hundred before quitting. During this process, an acquaintance suggested I apply for a grant and assured me that a trip to the library would give me leads and make self-publishing a reality. It did.

A note of special appreciation goes to Lisa Fedy who corrected and prepared the earlier manuscript. Many thanks to Debbie Leighton and the Advisory Board of the Eleanor Humes Haney Fund, for the grant that they awarded me that covered the expense of contracting a professional editor, Sylvia Sims of *Crone Graphics*. Additional thanks go to my fiscal agent, Gloria Hall, President and Coordinator of the *Charles Huston Cultural Project*.

Thanks also to Deborah Benner of **Goose River Press,** who opened the gate to publication, first offering to print the memoir if I chose to self-publish and then by accepting and including a portion of the manuscript in the *Goose River Anthology, 2005*.

I continue to write and I am working on *The Roan*, a fictional, historical tale based upon the oral history of my great-grandmother, Mary Jane Lee. I am humbled, grateful and proud.

PREFACE

Prudence, economy and ingenuity were necessities of living in the nineteenth and early twentieth century New England. Women ran households with very little money, canning produce from backyard gardens, making jams from woodland berries and sewing clothing for themselves and their families. My black Yankee family was intense, realistic, and skilled in many areas but I was—and still am—slow to grasp most practical skills. Adults had little patience teaching me to embroider and crochet and, when I trod the treadle of our old Singer sewing machine, it went backwards and broke the thread or the needle.

I loved to daydream and often worried that my excitement about the world around me would show. At home, in school—anytime things got unbearable—I'd go away in my head and envision alternate scenarios to whatever was going on . . . or wonder about a ladybug on the wall. I began writing my diary when I was eight. It felt odd and out of place to delight in writing. No one in my family seemed to spend time writing and I was unaware that my mother wrote. After her funeral in September of 1977, I salvaged boxes of papers and old photographs from my mother's house as it was decided that her sister Evelyn should move into it. That house at 12 Ellen Street was the house I grew up in. Evelyn had no use for those papers, and when the old house at 6 Ellen Street (where Evelyn had lived) was torn down, I collected even more boxes of cards and letters and photographs. My own house had lots of space then, so some boxes sat undisturbed for years. My pack rat collecting began then and reoccurs as relatives die off and survivors want to get rid of all the "old stuff." I discovered Ma's journal when I went through boxes trying to make room for my growing collection of "old stuff." One tiny blue diary begins in her neatest script: *"This is the Adventures of Dot Lee."* It is dated July 2, 1927 and continues with: *"Said good-bye to the horrible past and have started on a trip to try for all that is good and great."* It details her stay in Leominster when she was married to Bill Perkins. She describes her work in the laundry and the many relatives and social events she enjoyed in Leominster. She mentions how well others are caring for her two children, Sonny and Lois, then it ends abruptly on her birthday, Monday, October 17, 1927. The remaining pages dated until the end of October are blank.

A larger, green Five Year Diary starts on Wednesday, January 1, 1936. She describes the weather as *"glorious"* while inside the house there's *"plenty of storm."* There's a daily entry from January until July of 1936. She chronicles the elements of her domestic disaster with my father, Herbert. I was stunned to read her wistful entries about him. It was easy to remember their acrimony during those few years we lived together and I'd forgotten that she truly loved him.

My maternal grandmother—Gram—married Elias Edward Francis Rickards, who was born in Boston,

Massachusetts in 1867. His family came from Guinea and proudly boasted of being free people. Gram—Laura Frances Washington Rickards—told us stories about her life and also her mother's life on the Fleming Plantation in Maryland. Gram was born in Charlestown, Massachusetts in 1875. During her childhood, the family moved about the state to Groton, Ayer, Pepperell, Boston and Hyannis.

Her older siblings had begun life in Maryland where the oldest son, George, had remained to help the plantation owners when great grandmother was granted her manumission papers. Those "freedom" papers had been sewn to her petticoat for safety.

As Gram aged, her stories became repetitive and predictable but I never tired of the retelling or the repetition. I memorized them just as my own preschool children would memorize *their* bedtime stories. If I omitted a word or skipped a page there were loud protests! In the process of writing my Grandmother's stories to preserve them for generations to come, my daughter suggested I tell my own life story.

***

Race and its ugly aspects have to be a part of my life story just as it was in my mother's and my grandmother's stories, but experiencing racism was not the most influential factor of my life. New England, the Great Depression, my parents and a great host of other relatives and friends shaped my innermost being, but I cannot pretend that color did not impact my life.

An element of fiction is necessary (as in all autobiography) when people are quoted in the retelling.

Unforgettable events that bring smiles or tears to my face are in fact, "recollections." The exact words were, of course, never committed to tape. This book is *my* view of reality. Some names have been changed to afford anonymity to people whose whereabouts are unknown to me at this time.

Some family members may argue with my interpretation of events that they also experienced. This worried me. I was greatly relieved when Audrey—the sister I grew up with—read my draft manuscript as I trust her and rely upon her honesty. She wanted to read more and our collective memories soon fueled recollections of other childhood events and details I had forgotten, such as the red candies we used for pretend lipstick when we went on train trips.

My grandparents shared their stories orally and often omitted painful or humiliating events. I cherish their stories, but it is now time to document my own. It is my responsibility. I grew up colored and my life reflects the distinctions an oppressive society imprints on people like me. My memoir insures that historians and antiquarian societies will have a written work that commemorates the lives of people of African descent. Children should not live their lives without having a reflection of themselves and their own people in meaningful records.

PART ONE

Growing Up with Family

CHAPTER 1

Colored of Course!

My life is colored by racism—the ordinary everyday kind, the socially unaware and the institutionalized. My family of origin on my father's side, the Barrows, put on airs and imitated the white upper-middle-class in order to cope with racism. They colored everything dusty rose, flaunting bourgeois affectations, moving through layers of oppression as if they already possessed all the rights and privileges of the white middle-to upper-class. It worked. Their masquerade became as real to others as their role-playing had become to them.

My father's sister Helen sang on the radio. This was related to me as an amazing thing—a colored woman, singing for a big audience that included white people. (It may have been during the Works Project effort in the '30s to employ artists.) I imagine Helen in presenting herself, auditioning on the telephone. Her talent could be judged without exposing her color. Even today I use the telephone whenever I want to avoid the possibility of pre-judgment.

Her sister, my aunt Eulidia, required all delivery people to enter through the back kitchen door while my father, Herb Barrow, boasted of going to Harvard University. This declaration earned him instant admiration from both white and colored listeners. My mother

1

believed he was a student, but later found out the truth: he delivered dry cleaning there. *His* father, who left his wife and children to go home to Bermuda, had set my dad up in business. The actual Harvard students were good paying customers. Herb enjoyed vacationing on Oak Bluffs and he closed shop for the summer, spending his profits on Cape Cod. Inevitably, the business failed. Herb found opportunity next with Uncle Sam and spent many years in the First Battalion of the 372nd Infantry and in the National Guard. He became skilled in arguing cases and an expert in military law working in the Adjutant General's Office. His arrogance, his foresight and cunning, along with his photographic memory and Catholic upbringing, fueled his ambition. Why else would a white court judge be intimidated and tell my mother he could not issue a warrant on Captain Barrow for nonsupport? The judge and the Captain served in the National Guard together. Captain Barrow was a good officer and a gentleman— and in uniform he outranked the judge. Herb retired a Colonel to live a full, comfortable life as if he were a successful lawyer.

My mother's side of the family was colored in the way that house slaves had set themselves apart from field slaves. The Washingtons were freckled, both fair and dark skinned, towheaded, redheaded, and stood taller than their measured heights. The free Guinea men of the Rickards clan into which my grandmother had married, accused their son of marrying down— marrying the daughter of a house slave.

"No spirit in them," they accused. "Just colored folks acting white 'cause they lived with 'em and suckled their babies! Free men from Guinea would never

2

submit to such indignities as living with white folks!"

The new Mrs. Rickards—my grandmother Laura Frances Washington—defended her position well. She took every opportunity to be educated, spoke confidently, and gained access to all opportunities that her U.S. Citizenship afforded. To her, the door to success was a good education.

"Free schools and dumb niggers, it's a shame, a pitiful shame!" Mrs. Rickards would lash out at anyone who dared accuse her of ignorance. She'd declare "You'd better use the good sense that God has given you!"

I was schooled in ways to detect racist behavior and told how to deal with name-callers.

"You beat them or I'll beat you!" The warrior women that both my mother and grandmother had become put both spoken and unspoken demands on me. It was difficult for me to believe that racism could be so cruel, so pervasive. I watched for clues, held onto their advice and tried to remember tactics; I was instructed on how to be armed and ready to confront racism and this advice was often repeated.

"You'll have to work twice as hard to get half the recognition."

"You can do anything you set your mind to."

"They'll notice *your* mistakes before anyone else's."

"Get an interview by filling out your application properly, and where it asks for race, put a capital C. They'll think it's for Caucasian, and you won't be eliminated before they lay eyes on you." They knew all of the subtle signs of racism.

"If they don't put your change in your hand . . . if they wait on someone else and you were there first . . .

if they leave the seat on the bus or trolley next to you empty and stand. . . when they call you by your first name only." There were more. I didn't want to believe any of it. I would doubt and question.

"People aren't really like that," I'd say as I cringed at the thought of such things happening to me.

"Oh yes," they would assure me, "and you have to watch out when dealing with your own! They'll give you the cheapest and save the best for their white customers. They'll cheat you and think nothing of it, make appointments and not show up. You can't rely on them."

My adult relatives painted my entire view of the world for me. I was a colored girl and people noticed right away. I wasn't pale enough to pass. I couldn't hide. Someday I would be out in the wide world, having to accept that I would never be "free, white and twenty-one." I had realized by the time I started school, that Colored is forever.

CHAPTER 2

Blue Crib

My mother's voice penetrates my earliest memories. In my recollections there are not many people around, just sounds and isolated images. I peeped out between bars of a blue crib. It was a shadowy view, but I could see the floor clearly. It was bare, shiny wood. I was not sleepy, but chose not to move or make a sound. I perched on my hands and knees. (That position still brings me a feeling of comfort.) It seemed that I was alone except for muffled sounds drifting into my space. Sounds of footsteps clomping on wooden stairs and tumbling, clattering glass, assured me that someone was out there.

Are they coming in? No, they never come into my space. I lie on a knobby quilt with pale yellow and blue shapes. Night and day are the same. I am sick and no one comes to take me out of my crib. It feels good to crouch on my knees, rest my head on my arms, peep at the world and wait.

Mother told me our house was on Putnam Avenue in Cambridge. It was 1932.

"The apartment at number 149 Putnam Avenue was above a store. It was infested with roaches! I just sprayed every day with Flit until they stopped coming up. No one has to live with roaches." Her tone was

5

accusatory when she spoke about her triumph over the roaches. It was as if she was a cut above other folks who simply tolerated the nasty critters. We talked about my recollection of noise.

"No, our apartment wasn't noisy. It was the back apartment that was noisy. Narcotic agents raided their place, smashing all their bootleg liquor. You were just a baby. I don't know how you could remember that, but you babies *were* sick. Audrey and you both had whooping cough when we lived there. My sister Elsie sent your cousin Rainy to give me a hand. Rainy wasn't much of a mother's helper—just a teenager. I spent my time worrying about her and wondering where she was. She'd be down the street, hanging on some friend's gate, no help at all. I put Audrey into Nursery School. That was a help. She wanted to go to school and it was just down the street. I got her enrolled because she was so smart, and they let her stay even after the doctor examined her and knew she wasn't two years old. He noticed her milk teeth weren't in yet." (That term was Ma's way of describing Audrey's 2-year-old molars.)

My father grew up in Cambridge, and my sister Audrey was christened at Sacred Heart Roman Catholic Church while we lived there. Those are all my memories of Putnam Avenue.

CHAPTER 3

The House on the Hill

It is my house, or will be. It is a tall box sitting near piles of dirt, wood, and stones. I sit in a carriage that is a buggy-like a chair. The bottom half could drop down. It is not for babies. I sit up tall wearing my pink and blue knit tam. Sometimes when my aunts visit, they smile and ask me, "What's your name?" I answer, "Barrow." They laugh. How dumb they seem to ask that question. They already know my name.

I watch them build the house on the hill. One day my sister climbs the ladder to the top of the house. Bill LeBlanc—a man who is helping my parents—sees her, quiets my mother and goes up to walk Audrey down backwards. The other LeBlanc is his wife Florence, and they have a little girl named Tootsie. Tootsie is wild. She doesn't talk and she bites Florence on her knees. We live in Cambridge, but this is Worcester and just down through the tall grass you can see Gram and Grampa's house. They are my Ma's mother and father and they don't come up to the house on the hill. My mother goes down to their house and my father isn't around much. Grownups call my mother Dorothy and she and Florence and Bill pull nails out of wood, bang rocks and stay out in the sunshine. The LeBlancs don't look like me but they are like family. It is warm outside. Something has hap-

pened in Cambridge. We can't live there anymore but the house on the hill isn't finished yet, so we can't live there either, not now. We are going to a place called Sharon.

***

The house is still there, but it doesn't look anything like it looked in the thirties. It's beautiful now and a little boy named Marcus lives there. His mother, Dorothy Ellen, is my niece, named after her two grandmothers—Dorothy, (my mother) and Ellen, her dad's mom.

CHAPTER 4

Aunt Sister's

That winter in the house in Sharon, Massachusetts, everyone looked like me.

The house is a vivid memory, a picture I could draw on paper now, and paint it as well. We went in past the French doors with the sparkling glass knobs and up the wide staircase to the top of the house to our room. My mother hung our wash over the long wood railing that ran down the hall outside the room. That railing kept us from falling down the stairs and it wound around at the end and became a wide banister that looked like a perfect slide.

It was so cold! My mother held our nightdresses near the heater and I quickly pulled off my dress and petticoat, then I could feel the heat for just a moment before I began to shiver. The round stove showed yellow light through diamond shapes around the middle and cloverleaf shapes near the top. It was like a tall black hat, almost as tall as I was.

"My nightie, I'm ready for my nightie," I said.

"Take off your undies. I'm going to finish the wash."

I was quick. Off they came.

"Yikes! My flesh snapped as it stuck to the side of the heater. "Ouch!"

"Oh no, look!" my sister cried, "you've got a diamond

on your behind!"

It's funny how a person can hurt, cry and laugh—all at the same time.

"Wahh, ow, ow." I howled a bit more. The tears fell as the nightie was popped over my head. Arms enfolded me as I wriggled and almost giggled. I had a perfect diamond on my butt.

***

It is always winter in Sharon, there at dad's sister's house. Her real name is Eulidia or something ugly like that. That's probably why they call her Sister. No-one has any money. All our stuff is in a place called storage. I wish we could stay downstairs and sit at the big table with the Drummond kids. They are my cousins. Paul is almost the same age as my sister and me. I guess we can't play together since Paul got Audrey hurt. I am sure glad I wasn't holding the bottle while he pitched rocks at it. Paul has a good aim. It was the bottle popping that cut Audrey's hand open. Aunt Sister sticks Audrey's hand in cold water. My mother yells:

"What's happened? What happened to Audrey?" Sister doesn't say a word. Paul runs off somewhere. Audrey doesn't make a peep. Ka thunk! Sister, looking pale and gray, drops in a pile in front of the sink; down she goes in a heap on the big black and white squares. Audrey, still standing on a stool, looks down at Sister. The sink is red with blood and a basin of blood is hiding Audrey's hand. My mother stretches Aunt Sister out and lays her out like a big ugly doll. I can't stand Sister. I think maybe she's dead.

"Oh mama, mama," Audrey starts to howl as if she

had killed Sister. I've seen enough. I run past the French doors and don't look back. I miss the bandaging, but somebody does something to make Aunt Sister alive again. Everybody is talking. Now it's time to cry. Paul hurt my sister; now we can't play together and we have to stay in that cold room on the top floor.

One time we do get to play outside. It's been snowy, the rain freezes on top of the snow, and we can walk on top without sinking down. Our ski pants zip and slither when we slide down the hill on the bumpily crust. We go as fast as anything down the hill. We finish a great slide and are trying to get back to the top near the house. It's extra slippery from all that sliding and our boots are zipping and zapping and slip-sliding. There's a noise right behind us.

"Crack, crack, crunch, crunch, thump, thump!"

It gets louder and I hear huffing and panting! Audrey turns first and then we both see it: big and black with big horns, huge red eyes and smoke shooting out of its giant nose. It comes up the hill just behind our slipping feet! I try to grab the crusty snow. I'm on my hands and knees now and can't stand up!

"Help, help us! Oh help!" We can only move about an inch and it is still coming, crashing through the snow and ice. Somebody hears us, but they are laughing! Why are they laughing? Don't they see the danger? I scream for help. My throat squeezes with pain from trying to scream as my mouth is crying hard from somewhere down in my chest. Then I am up in the air, under some tall person's arm, dangling from my middle with my hands and feet flopping. I see Audrey across the coat's belly, under the other arm. I'm not sure, but I can still hear crying. We are alive! I can't stop crying. My heart

11

hurts and I just can't stop crying.

Sisters in Winter Coats

CHAPTER 5

Tainted

My early days had one dimension: still scenes—like black and white photographs—touched only by color where there were flowers or other wondrous things that simply won't fade from memory. Racism was like that back then: a tint and a brush stroke applied to an isolated event.

There was a day when my sister and I were all dressed up in navy blue, double-breasted coats. The coats had gorgeous gold buttons with anchor designs. My mother used to dress us alike, so people would presume we were twins. We were outside City Hall on Main Street in Worcester and something festive was happening. There was an organ-grinder with a tiny, nervous monkey on a short leash. Music that my mother called hurdy-gurdy music filled the air. A little girl walking with her mother came near us and the child pointed at my sister and me.

"Look, mama. Look! Twin monkeys! Oh *look!*" The small girl tried to pull her mother closer. She was excited and happy, but her mother tried to shush her and began to move away. My mother walked us towards the smiling girl, ignoring the adult.

"These are my daughters," my mother said, "they are little girls just like you." She stretched out her arms, proudly displaying her honey-brown hands. "They're my little girls"—my mother was beaming—"and they look just like me." The face of the little girl's mother has vanished from my memory, but I do remember that the little girl, my own mom and my sister and I fixed smiling eyes on one another until the little girl was pulled out of our sight. After that incident I began to notice color.

CHAPTER 6

Jan's Grandchildren

Roosevelt School on Grafton Street in 1934 was a new, cream-colored stucco elementary school. It was beautiful. A talented man maintained the meticulously groomed lawns and heart-shaped bayberry hedges. He was also a prize-winning animal breeder with many ribbons won at state fairs and expositions such as the Big E in Springfield. He was known as Jan Rickards, the Silky Man of Worcester and he was my maternal grandfather. Jan was a nickname, used affectionately by those who knew and loved Elias Rickards, the Janitor. I called him Grampa. While he lived, Roosevelt School was a special place. It had one of the few telephones in the neighborhood and before I was old enough for school, I went to Roosevelt to help clean and ready the building for fall. It smelled of wood and sweet oil.

In the 1930's, before my Hampton cousins moved to the other side of town, they helped my Grandfather clean the school. My sister Lois, who is the surviving child from my mother's first marriage to Bill Perkins, remembers going to Roosevelt School with Grampa. Later it was my turn, along with Audrey (the sister I grew up with) and my mother. I rode in a red wagon with real rubber tires with white rims, which was big enough to hold me, along with buckets, mops, rags, and boxes of cleaner. Roosevelt was close enough to my house that, when the woods went up in flames, my mother got Grandpa's keys and ran all the way to the school to call the fire department. Years later, we had a firebox on the light pole down at the corner of Grafton Street.

School was an exciting place. When my Grandfather told me he could look up the furnace smokestacks at midday and see the stars, I wasn't sure if it was true. But I felt really good about that furnace.

***

There's a story they read in Kindergarten. I would start school soon, but I didn't worry about the implications of the story because my Grampa was in charge of that school.

"Once upon a time there was a little boy named Sambo," Miss Squires is reading.

"Hey, Sambo, you got butter on your head?" Sometimes it is just a whisper—usually one of the boys. Then another kid calls out real sneaky. My mind freezes: black boy, tiger's stripes and pancakes. It always makes my stomach get queasy and I won't look at anybody. I don't want to hate them so much I can't ever play with them and I don't want 'em to think that the water swimming in my eyes would really drop down my face.

I just keep walking in the circle. We are supposed to be acting out the story or making it a game. Miss Squires never hears the name-calling. I don't even cry when I tell my mother.

I still get to clean the school in the summertime. My mother and Grampa laugh about how many Little Black

Sambo books get lost every summer. I wash the walls down low where my Grampa can't reach. Ma washes up high, 'cause he doesn't climb the ladder any more. He oils the wooden floors. My sister and me clean all the toilet stalls, wash all the inkwells, and scour the stains around the hole where the little glass wells drop into the desks. I flip the gray slate lids, one side opens the hole, and then slides back so no dust or eraser rubber can fall in. Every inkwell is shining before I pour in the fresh ink from a copper pot with a long snout. It is a great place; the big auditorium has a stage with giant flags on each side. There is a straw couch you can lie down on to wait for the nurse, big chunky wooden building blocks, a shiny black piano and best of all—a big furnace that can burn bunches of just about anything!

Newly Built Roosevelt School: Before Jan Rickards

CHAPTER 7

Poetry

It came from my Mother—
(Gram would also brag of parsing sentences
and reciting rhymes in school).
Ma knew astrology and mythology—
peering at the sky and naming the stars,
to tell about the gods of thunder and of the sea.
Oh how she could enchant—
spin a yarn, tell a tale, recite a poem,
to enthrall me.
The stories read in character,
poems rising and falling low then loud
in cadence and in fervor,
misty, mystical-
Abou—hmmm—*Abou Ben Adhem*
(*may his tribe increase*). . . .
A legacy on loan to me
a lifelong lease to own forever—
Poetry!
Sharing feelings, thoughts,
records, even history between us.
Lullabies, images of butterflies
nature, nurture, toil and torture.
The ugly, the mean,
Anything ever known or seen
real; imagined, made up, memorized.
There are no limits,
to poetry!

Gram & Grampa Rickards

CHAPTER 8

People and Places

Where I grew up was very different from the East Side where my cousins lived. My mother lived on the West Side near Beaver Brook when she was a girl. She left Malden to come to Worcester in 1914 where her family lived at 3 Hudson Place until 1921, then moved to 19 Rodney Street. My mother spoke about the West Side in longing tones. She had been a member of a group of young people of color who had fun together at picnics and dress-up socials at Beaver Brook Park. She was a teenager when she moved out to Ellen Street, the place my cousins called, "the country."

A year after living on Rodney Street, the family moved to 4 Ellen Street and two years after that, her father bought land and built a temporary home at number 6 Ellen Street. Ellen Street is a dirt street off Short Street at Sunderland Road that was home to me. For a short time my cousins lived out in the country too, on Niles Street next to Ellen Street.

Other places made me curious, but I knew everyone on Ellen Street and every adult acted like a parent. Grampa Millett, my next door neighbor, called me "girlie." He gave us garden surplus such as fresh tomatoes in season, and introduced me to hardtack with jam. I ate apples from his yard, admired his sculptured

Dorothy Lee Rickards, Teenager

catalpa trees, and his wife's flower garden. Grampa Millett pruned his Catalpa trees in the shape of umbrellas. I have a Catalpa tree in my yard today. They have large, fragrant white blossoms that yield long bean-pod shaped seeds.

My neighborhood was thickly wooded, with farms on both sides of Sunderland Road. Mark Hayes' pasture was our back yard. Just a short walk on the dirt path, through the sweet fern and I was at the stonewall that enclosed his grazing land. The Perkins' farm abutted Mark's land and went for miles into deep woods close to the Millbury town line. Horses romped on their farm and they had a large apple orchard. A few houses were tucked in near the farms, but most houses lined Grafton Street and were single-family homes. It seemed as if I knew every family and they knew me. I was one of Captain Barrow's daughters, or Jan Rickards' grandchild or one of the twins. My sister and I became known as the twins because my mother dressed us alike. Ma sewed stuffed animals from patterns on yard goods, crocheted lace on handkerchiefs, made fancy lace doilies, then sent us "twins" out into the neighborhood to sell her wares. When I grew taller we became a convincing duo. There were several families in the area who did have twins—the Magliaro family had a couple of sets of them. We never told people we were twins, but purposely did not refute their assumption. After all, part of every year, near the end of October to mid November, my sister Audrey and I *are* the same age!

There were several grocery stores on Grafton Street. Teddy's Market was on the corner of Grafton Street and Sunderland Road. Kersis's Store was on Grafton Street, just past Roosevelt School. The storekeepers and other adults I knew watched out for me and did not hesitate to reprimand me for any behavior they deemed dangerous. On icy roads, the weight of two kids on one sled made us rocket down hills, clacking and crushing slick trails on the way. One storekeeper, Russell Wellwood, snatched me off my sled as I crossed Grafton Street intending to slide down to Lake Avenue. He threatened to tell my mother if he ever saw me attempting that exhilarating feat again.

The woodlands were my playgrounds. I spent hours at Mark Hayes' farm, searched for frog's eggs, caught pollywogs in the pond and knew every edible berry, tree-bark and leaf. I walked to Lake Quinsigamond and often delighted in taking a forbidden swim. Jerry Oliver worked at Teddy's Market. He was not as fatherly as Russell, but Jerry's mother would call out to us kids, beckon us to her door and give us hot pizza. Adults called her Jigomene. Like many of our neighbors, she spoke little English, but I had no problem understanding her gestures. The pizza was made of thick, crusty bread dough spread with fresh, sweet, tomato sauce. No cheese.

CHAPTER 9

Seasons of Childhood

In the nineteen thirties, the pace of life seemed slower. There was no hurry to grow up. I played with dolls until I was in junior high and "fun" meant being outdoors playing games or sledding or skating.

Collecting frog's eggs, watching them grow into pollywogs, playing jacks, jump rope and marbles were the signs of spring turning to summer. Finding a nice, smooth duck—a flat oval stone—for hopscotch was another spring ritual.

As the neighborhood children on the hill got older, we stopped playing marbles in the spring but I held onto my hopscotch "duck," hoping the girls might want to play. When the ground dried out, all the young kids built roadways in Grampa Millett's garden plot and we would drive toy cars around the mini-highways. The ground yielded to shaping and every child could make mounds and turns or bridges and tunnels. Once the ground was plowed, that game was over and the older kids' games were tough. Pig-pile was popular, but when I was on the bottom it just felt like a fast way to die. Football was rough and my hand got clobbered the one time I was allowed to hold the ball for someone else to kick, but green apple wars were the worst. I couldn't throw straight. My grasp was too tight and I held on too long. If I chose to play with the gang in early summer after a windstorm, I learned fast to stay out of sight or I'd be sure to get welts all over my body. Hide and Seek was OK, but we had to go in when the street lights came on, so I didn't get to play much kick the can or red rover once it got dark. "King of the mountain" was another killer game where the big kids stood on a mound and threw any contenders off into painful heaps as they tried to become "king." On Ellen Street, I wasn't always one of the game players.

My sister was one of the gang and they'd come into my yard and whistle for Audrey to come out and play. Audrey was a great shot in green apple wars. If she got beaned, you'd never know it. She could climb trees, run like the wind and dodge better by far than most of the boys. Not being athletic, I ended up playing dolls on the porch with the smaller girls.

Summer felt as if it was a whole year away from school, and summertime was great! We kids would hop onto the wooden running board on the back of Todd's ice truck and bounce up and down as he drove up Ellen Street. He never minded the bunch of us and might even reward us with ice chips that flaked away as he chipped big ice chunks into custom-sized blocks. Todd wore a black rubber apron that covered him back and front. He would haul the ice chunks on his back, firmly grasped by big double-handled tongs. People put cardboard signs in their windows to request ice. The United Dairy milkmen, the TownTalk and Cushman Bread delivery men were also kind to children. The Upton Junk man traveled by horse and buggy and another traveling salesman repaired pots and pans and sharpened knives.

Every summer my sister and I would spend hours at Mark Hayes's farm. It was morbidly fascinating to watch him slaughter pigs. They would scream and squeal right to the end when Mark cut their throats. They were tied by their hind legs, hung upside down and lowered into a huge boiling cauldron of water that sat over an outdoor wood fire between the house and barn. On one occasion, our almost hypnotic focus was broken when we had to run for safety because one of the bulls got loose and was steaming toward the barn.

***

THE OCEAN

Summers, before Gram's sister Carrie died, were always fun because the whole family went to her house in Hyannis. It was one of those times in life when I could completely trust the world around me. They were pauses: places where no one cared I was colored. The ocean was one of those places. My Aunt Carrie lived on Cape Cod, right off Sea Street in Hyannis. She was my maternal grandmother's most freckled sister. We visited Carrie's home on Oak Neck Road every summer until the World War II years—that's when she died. Carrie had married an Indian named Ben Pocknet who I never met. They supposedly had one little girl who had died in a barn fire attempting to save her puppies. Relatives did not talk about it.

My mother was different when she was on Cape Cod; she didn't seem to worry. She had other grownups

Aunt Carrie Pocknet

to talk to which allowed her to free us. Gram went with us and sometimes Aunt Evvie came too. The women relaxed and we girls went off to the beach. I often spent the whole day at Sea Street Beach, a pleasant walk from the house. We strolled down sandy-edged black-top roads lined with scrub pines, beach plums and the scratchiest grass God ever created. It was heaven. I can't remember a day that was cold or rainy or dull. There were brief showers, after which I'd drag my hand along the white-blossomed privet hedges, delighting in the sprinkle of droplets and the sweet smell the bushes would give out. On rare occasions we bought potato chips at a small store up on Sea Street. There was always popcorn at the house and tiny red ants would find their way into the sealed bags and tins but, no matter, everyone ate the popcorn.

Mother always advised us girls, "You watch out now. If it looks like someone's going to give you trouble, you hold hands and run. When you walk home from the beach, put a handful of sand in each pocket. If somebody in a car tries to bother you, just pitch that sand their eyes and get on home quick!"

We never did meet anyone who gave us trouble. To the contrary, some people were especially thoughtful. One man kept watching us as we played in the sand. The sunshine beamed down, deeply coloring our skin as we sweated and so we cooled off by jumping into the ocean and found some big wooden logs to hold onto. We could not swim but the buoyant salt water bobbed us around like corks. I had no fear of the water, so no sense of alarm rose in me when the two of us drifted out to sea. The man had been swimming near us all afternoon. His vigilance brought him way out beyond all the other bathers as he gently towed the log to the shallows.

"You girls were way out over your heads. You be careful now, OK?"

We *were* more careful. Nothing bad happened to us, but there was a war going on in Europe and Aunt Carrie got sick and died. It was 1944 or '45. Aunt Carrie had to go to the hospital. There was something different about that hospital in Pocassett because we never got to visit her there. Maybe she had consumption and that's where they brought you when you were infectious.

Summers on Oak Neck Road ended for us after they waked Aunt Carrie. The coffin was right there in the parlor. I watched Aunt Elsie and other relatives adjust Carrie's dead body. They repositioned her hands, fussed with her dress and moved her flowers around. It was sickening to see Aunt Carrie dead and those women fussing with her. God, what were they thinking? I got a raging fever and was put to bed up in the attic loft.

From the loft's small window I saw people sitting on folding chairs near the back door. They weren't singing but the strange wailing sounds they were making were like moans from a far-off place. It was *hot*. The strange women I saw were huge; fanning themselves and sweating. They wore white dresses with blood-red flowers pinned to their bulging chests. I just flopped down in my bed and cried. When it got dark the air felt cool. It was deathly quiet when I came downstairs and peeked into the parlor. They were all gone: my cousins, the moaning women and Aunt Carrie too.

"My, my, she was so feverish this morning. She's

31

certainly fine now," my mother seemed pleasantly amazed.

There was a final Cape Cod visit when the house was emptied. They used a friend named Gordon's truck. After it was loaded, Aunt Evvie sat up front and my sister and I got to ride in the back with all the stuff. They trucked it up to Worcester where it ended up at 6 Ellen Street, my Grandma's house. After all, Carrie and my Grandma were sisters. Carrie didn't leave a will and those many Cape Cod cousins felt they should inherit Carrie's house. Lawyers tried to get them to sign off the house to Carrie's living brother and sister, Laura and George. They wouldn't. The Irish neighbor across the street thought it was a pity that my Gram didn't get the house and the lots when it was all sold off at public auction. That neighbor was the highest bidder. Out of the several generations of children the Washington siblings had had, no relative possessed enough savings to bid.

Gram used to say, "Every Washington on the Cape—and there were plenty of them—got two dollars apiece. What a shame!"

***

DROPS

Summers were good, but autumn was the best! These were exciting times when color only mattered as a thing of beauty and autumn was a beautiful time. Going back to school stirred up some excitement and worry, but what made me feel important and special had to do with the "drops." By mid-September it would

Twins in Halloween Costumes

happen: the leaves on the berry bushes turned flame-red and yellow sassafras leaves danced in the breeze. The apple trees in the Millett's yard bore more fruit than they could harvest. The winds got blustery and the old folks talked about hurricanes. Ripe apples fell to the ground and got crushed by cars or stomped on. My house was nearer to Mark Hayes' farm than any of the other children's, so I got the greatest enjoyment from it. Mark's cows caught the smell of apples on the breeze and the herd would gather at the stone wall. Sometimes I would hear them bellowing as they tried to climb over the wall and when there were adult bulls in the herd, they'd eventually dislodge some stones. I would stand on the path in the woods and feel it begin to tremble, then the ground would shake and a muffled sound like far-off thunder would reach my pricked ears. I'd wait on the path until I saw the first big, red-eyed cow galloping down to the apple trees.

"The cows are coming! The cows are coming!" My voice was never stronger and my legs could move like the wind itself, getting me safely up onto Millett's back steps before the herd reached the house. It was the greatest sight, all those big black and white cows bolt-ing into the yard. Mark would have to come, rope the oldest bull or lead cow and walk them all up the road to the barn. His pigs and horses sometimes ran away too, lured by the wonderful fall odor of apple drops. It was the best time of the year and my birthday came in October too!

***

Halloween was special, even though we did not trick or treat in a formal way. What made it fun was the mischief that happened when groups of kids came down from Grafton Square. They would skillfully throw rocks and break all the street lamps from the square to Sunderland Road. The lamps were large bulbs, topped by fluted tin reflector shields. I was only a watcher when, in the darkness, garbage pails were tied up on flagpoles and cars waxed. But, when it came to raiding gardens, I joined in. I couldn't throw straight, but I could run fast. One person would run through the garden and kick cabbage heads off; I'd grab one and head for home. Ma cooked great smothered cabbage. It's amazing to me now that she never asked where the cabbage came from and equally amazing that, after being chased by dogs and angry gardeners, I never got caught.

***

In winter I loved skating, even though my laces would freeze and I would have to walk home in my skates. I loved being the kid on the end when the big kids played snap the whip. We'd be in a line, holding hands and skating fast. Then the first lead-kid (usually a boy) would stop, dig his skate firmly into the ice like an anchor—and the rest of us literally flew! Often I'd end up in a snow bank off the ice. Sledding was everyone's passion. Big storms would make Sunderland Road the longest ride imaginable. We'd start way past the school and slide right across Grafton Street to Lake Avenue. It was pure fun despite dealing with frost bite, chilblains, and wool ski pants reeking of pee. I tried ski-

35

ing, but didn't have real skis until after I was grown.

***

FREE, WHITE AND 21

I wanted my grandchildren to stand on my shoulders to gain a more accurate perspective on life. When I noticed my youngest grandson's captivation with a book series called *Box Car Children,* I wondered if there were people of color in any of the adventures. Gertrude Warner, the author, wrote the stories in 1918 when she was a substitute teacher. By 1942 there were many new versions of the same imaginary family. Her main characters, Henry, Jessie, Violet and Bennie Alden, were white children who never encountered black children in their adventures. Will there ever be a time when he will see a reflection of himself? I was determined not to let my grandchildren go through life burdened by the weight of invisibility. Except for Little Black Sambo and references to a character named Topsie, I couldn't remember any storybooks that included anyone in my image. In essence I was told to negate my own existence, so I longed for a time when I could see main characters that looked like me. When I bought books for the grandchildren, I made sure that some of the main characters looked like them. My daughters read voraciously, had favorite authors, and sought works by black writers when they reached school age. Black consciousness was being raised in their time, the sixties.

This phenomenon of the lack of positive black characters *could* explain why—as a little girl in the thirties—I loved white dolls and blonde wigs. White was my only

Dorothy and Elsie Rickards and Doll

image of acceptability and of beauty. Villains wore black hats, Africa was the "Dark'"continent and if one had a picture of happiness or success, it was displayed on a white face.

Every Christmas when I was very small and we were living in just the one room at Ellen Street, a miracle would happen. We had the black cast iron stove then, and we ate, slept and played in the tarpaper-wrapped space on the lower south side of the unfinished house. There wasn't always a tree, but for years Mother would bring out the small blue artificial tree with its fold-up branches. We made gifts for our grandparents: dates, pit removed and replaced with half a walnut or filled with peanut butter, then rolled in granulated sugar. We would wrap them up in small boxes and make them as pretty as jewels. We might get a hoped-for orange in our stockings. Mother still used to recite poetry then and she could tell any story with such realism, I believed she must have written it herself. I loved listening to Dorothy recite poetry.

"You better not pout and you better not cry . . ." There must have been something in that poem about peeking but—try as might—could never stay awake long enough to catch Santa performing the magic.

My sister and I each had a doll. They were beautiful white dolls with eyes that closed when the doll was laid down. They had real eyelashes and gorgeous long hair that would be braided, brushed, curled and crowned with clover blossoms or dandelions, so that by the year's end, the dolls were nearly bald. The wigs were cemented on and withstood water. Miraculously, at Christmas, Mother would buy new wigs and attach them securely on Christmas Eve. Sometimes she was

38

able to buy doll's shoes and socks and more than once, she would crochet clothes for them too. Some years the clothes came in packages, and some other years, hand-made ones came from my aunts who worked in garment shops in Boston.

"Now leave your doll near the tree. Santa is coming tonight!"

My fervent Christmas wish was to get the blonde wig. That's when I first came to accept my invisibility in a white world, so I planned at age twenty-one to become not only of an age to make decisions and take power, but to exist as a real person: free, white and twenty-one. I had learned patience at that young age and so clung to hope in order to make any current misery just a challenge on the way to becoming—becoming all that I knew I could be. After all, I was used to miracles.

I would wake up early Christmas morning trying to catch a glimpse of Santa, but what I saw was my old doll, all dressed up in new clothes and crowned with a new wig! I always hoped it would be the blonde wig. It was okay if it wasn't, because those dolls looked divine—and maybe next year, I *would* get the blonde one.

CHAPTER 10

Delights and Dilemmas

There *were* many delights; like our summers on Cape Cod and train rides to Boston. Those treasured moments and days softened the all too frequent hard times. A small gift of candy to enjoy on the train heightened the whole adventure. They were special candies: red ones that looked like big M&M's in a small cardboard cylinder. You could use them to paint your lips. We also had lollipops with soft, looping, twisted paper handles called Lallapaloops, which were smooth, flavorful, heart-shaped lollipops wrapped in clear cellophane with no stick to hurt your mouth if you bumped your face or fell.

Special foods were frequent pleasures. Grampa bought big vanilla and spice drop cookies from Brockleman's Market. They crowned up the middle and sometimes had one raisin on the peak. When Ma shopped at Worcester Market, we'd get a few groceries and then go up to the fruit store, the United Dairy; making one more stop before settling down at the Royal Movie Theatre. Kresge's Market sold wax-paper-wrapped hamburgers in warm soft buns. The hamburger was smothered in brown gravy with sautéed onions, garnished with a few thin-sliced, tender dill pickles. We ate them in the theatre. Nothing in the world tasted better than those hamburgers!

When my mother got a job on the Work Projects Administration my sister and I became the homemakers. Before she got the job, we had received commodities from welfare. There were tins without labels, corn meal and dried beans. Some large tins had stringy chunks of cooked pork and lots of the smaller tins had beets, making creativity essential. We didn't have to buy butter as we used blocks of white oleomargarine that came with small octagonal packets of red-orange dye.

Audrey and I once cooked a box of rice that swelled and swelled and spilled out of the pot onto the stove. We put it into more pots but it became quite a mess. Surprisingly, my Mother didn't even get mad. There were some food adventures that she didn't discover, such as the time we ate an entire jar of peanut butter. A spoonful at a time, we consumed the whole thing in one sitting. It was a two-pound, square glass jar with a honeycomb texture. I still like peanut butter and found a square jar with the same texture and I keep it as a sentimental treasure.

We'd often pick dandelions, split the stems and hold them in our mouths until they coiled into perfect long curls. The bitter taste was tolerable, but sometimes when we had a handful, we stuck them into the rain barrel. We used them to make wigs to crown our balding dolls' heads. Audrey made lovely mud pies decorated with dandelions. I ate them. As the years passed, my housekeeping and cooking skills improved and so did my taste in pies.

Long before my mother went to work and cooking became one of my jobs, I loved our kitchen. It was in the southwest corner of our square, ten feet by ten feet of living space. Ma had a high kitchen cabinet that she herself had painted in bright colors. The trim was royal blue and there were bright parrots she had hand painted in oils on the paneled doors. The cabinet had a large bin on the left where pounds of flour were poured in and stored and there was a sifter snout on the bottom of the bin. Other panels, also adorned with bright birds, fronted storage cupboards. There was a workspace under the paneled cupboards and the flour shoot. The white enameled surface could be pulled out to make a large tabletop where one could roll out and cut dough to make cookies, pies or biscuits. Our black, cast iron stove was another kitchen marvel. Its hot, shiny nickel trim was perfect for sculpting big icicles into creative shapes. We had a round icebox first then a square one with a flap near the floor for a drip pan; we didn't put a pan there because there was a hole in the floor that let the melted ice water fall to the ground. I could squeeze my wiry body into the hole on the outside and slide through the flap into the house.

Gram always cooked the Thanksgiving dinner and Audrey and I would go down to her house to help in hopes of speeding up the day-long cooking affair. Gram made savory fish chowder, oyster stew, succotash and codfish cakes; her corn chowder was scrumptious too. She would use the same big, round-bottomed aluminum pot and always started the chowders with finely chopped onions sautéed in a bit of oil from a scrap of salt pork. My sister had more patience than I possessed. She and Gram were early risers and went off into the woods together. That patience made both of them great berry-pickers too. Usually I sat at the first berry patch, picked, ate and waited for their return.

The women in the family were notably creative, but crafts were not my forte. Along with the feminine skills of sewing, knitting and crocheting, we were also taught to chop, saw, nail, shovel and haul. We had gardens and I had chickens to tend.

***

WORKING FOR A LIVING

I learned the necessity of earning money when I was young. The absence of money was harsh and even when my mother entered the work force my life did not become easy. When she went to work, Ma no longer would dance the fandango to entertain us. Her long, dramatic poetry recitations ended. I do not remember her reciting poetry after she went out to work. The poem I liked best was about Abou Ben Adhem. I would fall asleep before the poem ended.

Abou Ben Adhem (may his tribe increase)!
Awoke one night from a deep dream of peace
And saw, within the moonlight in his room
Making it rich like a lily in bloom,
An Angel, writing in a book of gold—
Exceeding peace had made Abou bold,
"What writest thou?" The vision raised its head . . . .[1]

[1]"Abou Ben Adhem," *The Book of Knowledge* 1945, 3-1138.

Gram Rickards on Mark Hayes' Wall

Ma recited it in a hushed, mysterious voice. I could clearly envision the Angel lighting Abou's room with a golden glow. The recitations ended.

The magic of her cooking was also gone forever. In the days before her jobs, she could take one egg, a few pieces of bread, a cup of milk, a pinch of flour and a dab of butter and make a meal for three. She made a thin white sauce, poured it on buttered toast, then sliced circles of boiled egg-white on top. Then she grated the hard-boiled egg yolk on top of each serving and presented us with a scrumptious, hot meal that she called goldenrod eggs. When my mother and her sisters worked at home, making hairbrushes from pig bristle, she was still her magical self. The women would talk together, but even when she worked alone, I could watch her create something that was wonderful from what seemed like nothing.

Her materials were on a box-like, small, narrow table. I watched her spin the vise that held the brush handle upright. She took a pinch-size bundle of bristle, fastened hair-thin wire around the center of the bundle, then pulled it through one of the many tiny holes in the top of the metal brush handle. She would continue to fasten each tuft until every hole was filled. Row after row, she would pull the wire snugly. She wore brown cotton gloves with the fingers cut off so the wire could be pulled tight without cutting her hands, while her finger tips selected uniform bundles of pig bristle. She would run her awl down each completed row to flatten the wire and produce a beautiful hairbrush that was so smooth that it would tickle the palm of your hand. Those same skilled fingers crocheted lace around the edges of handkerchiefs that I sold to our neighbors.

Mother with Hampton Kids Making Hairbrushes

Then she went to work for the Works Progress Administration. We lost the playful woman we called Ma.

***

WORKING AT HOME

I earned the first money from my own labor selling eggs. It was my job to tend the chickens and I worked diligently. In summer, I had help whitewashing the hen-house walls but, during the winter, I became less industrious and more dependent. Cleaning the hen-house became overwhelming. Frozen manure built up so badly that my sister would be pressed into service to help. Selling the eggs was the most rewarding part of the job and I had regular customers. I took pride in the amount of money I could get for a dozen double-yolked, jumbo eggs. Well fed, well cared for mature chickens laid big eggs.

I had several feisty roosters who spurred my legs, jumped on my back, and terrified me. I thought they would peck out my eyes. It seemed to entertain my sister to see me intimidated by stupid roosters. One rooster was enough to increase the flock so we ate most of them. Using them for food required special skills; chopping the head off a live, struggling chicken was the most difficult for me. We tried slaughtering chickens ourselves only once. Our neighbor, Mr. Liccardoni, usually did the deed for us. I think he knew just how to snap their necks! Another neighbor, Russell, used a knife and once cut himself badly.

We hung them in the cellar to drain, then plucked

the feathers and pinfeathers. After we singed the remaining hairs off the naked birds, we eviscerated them. I learned to do that well. I could identify anatomical organs and saw how they functioned, so cleaning the entrails was an intriguing chore. We stopped raising chickens in the 1940s.

***

FUN

We did the laundry, gathering up all of our wash and carting it down to Grandmother's house because she had electricity and a fat, white, round wringer-washer. The water came from her rain barrel. We had a rain barrel too and it was our secret swimming pool. On summer days we'd jump in and splash around. During a rain shower, we would climb into the barrel and stand under the rain spout, letting the water gush on our heads! Our dolls got to dive in, too!

One washday my hand went through the wringer with the sheet. It was up to my wrist before my sister reversed the direction. My ring was damaged beyond repair, but the hand just throbbed and stung for a few minutes.

The best thing about doing the wash was getting a chance to listen to Gram's radio. We followed the soap operas: *Our Gal Sunday, One Man's Family and The Guiding Light.* We would mimic the prologues and make up our own stories at bedtime, taking turns as narrator, cooperatively weaving the story line into nightly episodes. The adventure stories on the radio were great, too. By the time all the wash was done, wrung out, hung, dried and folded, we would have listened to *Renfrew of the Mounties, Henry Aldrich, I Love A Mystery or The Green Hornet.*

We never reported mishaps—such as my hand going through the wringer—to adults. Their fears and pre-occupations were more frightening than the hurts. We avoided the blame, shame and punishment that the adults always seemed to assign to accidents. We played commandos and jumped off shed roofs. We vaulted over fences, scaled walls and shimmied under fallen trees. I jumped off a shed, hit my chin with my knee and nearly knocked myself unconscious. It took a while before I could get up. Another jumping stunt gave me a nasty gash. I burst through a tin sheet covering a chicken run, cutting through my navy-blue knee sock and tearing a big gash below my knee. We pressed on it until the bleeding stopped and pulled the knee sock over the wound. I wore the same sock for more than a week, and then had to cut it off, leaving a strip of it in the scab that had formed. It soaked off weeks later in a Saturday night bath.

There were tiny roofs above gabled windows at 12 Ellen Street and an upstairs window opened onto one of those roofs. We used to put little rocking chairs on the roof and sit out there for fun. It scares me now when I look at that small, slanting roof. I don't know what kept us from tumbling off. We were gutsy, agile, creative children.

***

FEAR

My mother Dorothy's stories were many and exaggerated. Whether to teach, calm or warn, her stories were selected to meet her needs. Her rendition of the Three Little Pigs was customized to fit the occasion. When my father, Herbert, came to the house to demand dishes that had been their wedding gift, Ma surmised he was seeing another woman. She was right.

"He can huff and he can puff, but he'll never blow this house down!" Mother sent us little girls to safety in the bed under the wool army tent blanket. Banging and pounding on the door continued until the wood gave way, just above the knob. I remembered hearing screaming but always thought it was my sister's voice. I was too terrified to breathe, never mind scream.

"Oh no, oh no. Daddy broke the door!" I see my mother, baseball bat in hand poised to strike. Mother's voice is strong and I don't doubt for a second that her promise is good as done.

"You put your hand through this door and I'll knock it off."

The shouting stopped. A hand never came through the door, but Mother's stories about men always had a dark side. Men were all like the Big Bad Wolf, tricky, sly and out to get you!

***

CLAP

When she spoke about her first husband, Bill Perkins and their two children, Lawrence and Lois, she was always sad. Bill remarried a woman named Sally, who raised my sister Lois.

My father, Herbert, married five times! I knew all of his wives except the first. She had no children. My mother, Dorothy, was his second wife and she bore him three children. My parent's youngest girl, nine months younger than me, died in infancy. His third wife, Hazel, had a son, Thorton, who my father adopted when they married. We called him Bunkie. My dad's fourth wife, Emma, had a daughter, Linda, to whom my father gave his name. Her early records are all Barrow, but it seems it was not an "official" adoption. With wife number four my father had two more children who he called his autumn children: Herbert Junior and Anita who is named after his mother. He divorced all of his wives, then on the advice of his sister Anna, remarried wife number four so he would not be alone "in his old age."

"Bill was just like that—spoiled. I'd pack a lunch every day for him to take to work and off he'd go—to his mother's. He'd cry and she'd feed him."

There were appalling as well as sad parts to the "Bill" stories. One baby dies and another is given away. They were true stories; horrible, frightening tales that created scary images of black men for me.

"Foundry work is hard and dangerous. Those men worked with open fires and no protection. Bill only lasted a few days. He brought me home money just once. I tried hard to make those lunches . . . there just wasn't enough money but I did it every day. One time, I just had some lard and put it on bread."

I never asked, "What happened then?" or showed any kind of curiosity. This was a story I tried not to hear. There was never a part in it where I wanted to

Herbert Aaron Barrow & Wife #2:
Dorothy Lee Rickards Perkins Barrow

applaud. I simply waited, hoping the story would soon end.

". . . and after the next baby came, we were living right there next door to Gram and Gramps. It's just a cellar hole now. Jobs were harder and harder to find." My mother, Dorothy, never said, "for black men." I knew. My own father was out of work. We had had to leave Cambridge and spend that awful winter in Sharon.

"Porters don't make much money and after the crash, they got nuthin'! Bill worked the trains too. He rode them—a Pullman porter."

I thought a Pullman porter must be a better job than the Red-Cap kind of porter that my dad was. I had evidence that it was better as—even then—Bill, Ma's first husband, would give us passes to ride the train to Boston.

"Braaintree, Braaintree!" The conductor would shout the strangest things. My mind would wander to the best parts of remembering Bill. While my mother droned on about the horrors of marriage, I would put my mind in a happy-memory-place, like Union Station. It was a great place to clack your feet and to slump onto smooth, slithery wooden benches that were a mile long. There were people just everywhere! The big glass-covered hall echoed the voices of uniformed men up in the balcony, shouting out times of train comings and goings. I only remember going and coming to Boston.

It's choke-in-your-stomach scary when the trains fume in. I'm up on the platform. Somehow, we get upstairs and outdoors. Before you can hear the train, the ground begins to tremble, ever so little at first. The whistle screams like murder and wails all the way to the sta-

tion. Then comes the rumbling noise, pounding in rhythm like an angry beast, chugging louder and louder, then screeching as the big steel wheels begin shooting sparks! The gasping black train blows giant, steaming blasts that makes me wrap my face in Ma's skirt. It is truly awful and so exciting!

***

Fortunately, my mind could wander to thoughts more pleasant than my mother's lamentations.

". . . I was so swollen . . . the doctor stitched me up. Bill said I was too small, so he tore the stitches out. When he gave me clap, the doctor called him in. I didn't know what was wrong with me. I was so sick I nearly died. That's why I had to go away to get well again, up to my cousins in Leominster."

Dorothy told it all. Her eyes never met mine or she would have seen the frozen fear in them. She just had to tell someone. Any story about her life before marriage was always a reprieve.

"We lived on Hudson Place in a boarding house off Park Avenue when we first came to Worcester." (Dorothy's father was the villain in *these* reflections.)

"They didn't allow little children in the boarding house, but Evvie was such a cute, precocious baby, they let us stay until we found another house. Pa was still finishing jobs in Malden. He'd get a great job doing horticulture and landscaping. Then he'd teach the people who hired him how to do what he did and he'd be out of a job again. Living in the Chan-Ju-May area was just fine. There were socials at Beaver Brook and we had a grand time. Going to school was a problem at

54

first so Gram came and sat in our classrooms. They tried to make us go all the way down to Thomas Street School, but Gram said that Abbott Street is right here in our neighborhood, and she told 'em she'd keep us home if they couldn't see it her way. We did end up at Abbott Street. Gram saw to it.

"Thomas Street was rough. They tried to send all the colored there. The teachers would yell and even throw things. Big kids who couldn't speak English sat in those little third grade chairs. Gram had been through enough of the racial stuff in Malden. There, Gram would walk me 'n Elsie to school with a horsewhip in her hand. Those Irish kids would climb up in the trees and call us names; taunt us all the way to school. She could really wield a horsewhip! She got so she could pull 'em down right out'a the trees!

"We moved around Worcester to Rodney Street, and finally Ellen Street, number four. An Italian friend of Pa's helped him buy lots on Ellen Street. It wasn't easy to buy land on the high side of Grafton Street—there's miles of ledge here and the Swedes bought the prime land. No Italian immigrants were allowed. Gram wouldn't live in the lowland and feared those who did would get consumption."

I felt safe on the high side of Grafton Street. It must have been special for my mother, Dorothy, too when the Rickards family lived at number four Ellen Street. Ma not only talked about her good times there and at Beaver Brook, but there was also proof in the photographs of children that they had taken in, as well as lots of snapshots of smiling cousins plus a dog named Maggie. It seemed the dog had a face like Jiggs' Maggie of the comic strips.

It never took long after the good part of any story to get to the other, sorry part such as how her father got diabetes and dropsy and began to complain how his teen-aged daughters took away his privacy. Then she'd be back to telling why she left her happy home to marry Bill Perkins. There were never any compliments or praise for black men. Clap was a social disease festered by racism.

***

FIRE AND HEROES
December 1999

I think about the six fallen heroes: the ones who died trying to save people the police thought were squatting in the vacant Worcester Cold Storage building. That terrible catastrophe makes me remember my admiration for men dedicated to save people from fires. My first firefighter hero was Hector Birtz, Bobby's father who fell off a roof and died. It was doubly sad, because his wife Bertha never got a fireman's pension as he wasn't on duty when it happened. He died nearly sixty years ago when I was a schoolgirl and my heartthrob was the boy next door.

When the alarm rings and the fire is anywhere within running distance, Bobby, my sister and I go and watch. Bobby is immensely proud of his dad. I can feel it too—Bobby's dad is a hero! The fire alarms are on electric light and telephone poles. They are small, red, house-shaped boxes with a glass door. A tiny metal hammer attached by a chain is on the box where it is fastened, adult high, to the pole. You have to break the glass and pull the switch down. You stand right there because in a minute or two you hear the siren coming right from Posner Square. The fire engine howls up and down the slow hills of Grafton Street and you are the one to tell the chief exactly where to go. In the real olden days, my mom would run to Roosevelt School where there was a telephone, and call the fire department or the ambulance. That's what it is like in the early 1930's.

One time the fire is right by Cole's house at Trahan's field. Kids had skated there, just as I skate on Mark Hays' pond, but the field is now wetland, choked with reeds and fat cat-o'nine tails. Bobby knows his dad will be there and the three of us just know we can help. The gallant firemen whack down the flame in the weeds. Smoke and sparks fill the air. Hector Birtz is there. We can see him through the smoke. We are there alongside the firefighters. No one chases us away. When the engines go back to the station, Bobby, my sister, and me go to Bertha's. The fire is out and we are all sooty and singed, bursting with pride—because we helped Bobby's dad put out the fire!

***

HUMILITY

When ugly things happened at school, I put on my mask of indifference. There were ways teachers both pitied me and mortified me at the same time. The "absent" student's milk is one example: in the kindergarten, children were served milk and graham crackers or flat, thin, dimpled chocolate tea biscuits. Most children brought weekly milk money from home, so the teachers would assemble all those students who had paid in the auditorium, near the stairs to the office where the refrigerator stood and serve the snack. We did not have milk-money so, after they had returned to the classroom, I would be called out if someone who had paid was absent. The half-pint glass bottles were cold and the milk tasted wonderful, but a lump of humiliation crowded my throat. Like most children, I tried to hide my humiliation.

Ma would not let us go to school before the first bell. Her distress about the taunting and name-calling that we endured convinced her that we did not need any social time in the school yard. There was very little time between the first bell and the late bell; no matter how we pleaded, she held firm. That meant we had to run every step of the way to get to class before that second bell. Sometimes I would vomit my cereal; my sister threw up every day. I never got rattaned, but Audrey was rattaned once when we were late. A teacher or the principal used a wooden ruler to strike her open palms and her knuckles were whacked too. The next time that we were at the door and heard the late bell ringing, we did not go in, but went back home through the woods and hid in Gram's outhouse. We listened carefully for the sound of the opening of the porch door, then hid behind the outhouse until she went back inside. We stayed there all day until we heard the dismissal bell.

Our drinking water was stored in a four-quart aluminum teakettle. We melted snow in winter or carried water from Mark's pond; once we got the rain barrel, hauling water got easier. We did not drink the rainwater as sometimes we put a film of kerosene on the surface of the rain barrel to kill the mosquito larvae. Our neighbors, the Milletts, let us get drinking water from their outdoor spigot. One evening, when I was sent to carry drinking water from the neighbors, the voices inside sent me running, just running. The neighbors had company from Maine that evening. Grammy Millett's sister looked out at me from the kitchen window. (She looked just like Grammy Millett; Audrey told me later that her name was Ida and they were twins.)

"Ella! Ella!" She was pointing at me and yelling. "Oh, Ella, there's a pick-a-ninny stealing your water!"

I shut the faucet off and ran, and ran and ran. I couldn't face going home without the water. There was no way to explain to my mother what had happened. After the hot tears stopped, a burning knot stayed in my stomach. It was after dark when I carefully drew the water in a small, silent stream.

***

Silence and invisibility gave me a false sense of safety. Some children had a lot more courage than I did. My sister was one of them. No matter how Ma thrashed her, tied her up, blindfolded her, taped her mouth—she would not give any adult the satisfaction of seeing her cry. I would bellow for hours just at the sight of the horrible treatment she received. I overheard my mother tell my Grandmother,

"I'll break her spirit!"

Thank heaven, neither my mother nor the teachers at Roosevelt School ever did. The fear and horror of witnessing what happened to Audrey made me seek a place in the shadows. I grew up feeling that I did not have a place in the sun. It was safer, cooler, to be quiet, docile and as nearly invisible as a brown girl could be.

Other children at school made me feel proud of them but silently terrified me, too. Their courage amazed me. Betty Magnuson was one special friend who dared to choose me as a partner in a recess game. There was a chant to the game. We'd sing:

"Japaneedle, Japaneedle, I sew with my needle and when I get married I'll go to the garden and whistle and whistle and whistle for Shirley. Shake a day day, shake a day day, shake a day day farewell."

I was then greeted as I came into the square space set aside for the Japaneedle game and could chant and choose the next person. Occasionally after Betty's bravery, Evelyn Tully would imitate her and choose me. It did not happen often. Betty was a beautiful, fair-haired, blue eyed genteel girl. She walked with straight-backed pride, dressed beautifully and kept her blond hair impeccably in place. Every girl and boy admired her.

Eddy Nelson and Jimmy Mott were the scapegoats. Jimmy was sweet and gentle. Eddie was pudgy and kids tried to torment him by calling him Jumbo. I felt ashamed that I could not stand up for either of them, but not joining in the taunting was all the courage I could muster. I feared that if I defended Jimmy and Eddie, all the taunting and name-calling would come at me instead. Janey Robideau forced me into action. She was a great play pal—the tomboy type. On rare occasions my mother allowed us to play after school at Betty's house. She lived at 181 Sunderland Road, towards Rice Square. Janey lived in the neighborhood too and Cowboys and Indians was our favorite game. One day a group of us were walking home when a small cluster of older boys started name-calling. Janey joined in with them and I smashed her face as hard as I could. Red welts showed where I bopped her—even though her face was already scarlet. We both shed tears and knew our friendship was beyond repair.

Betty remained a true friend until her untimely death in January of 1941. Classmates were not allowed to see her. The cancer that wracked her body put ugly lumps on her beautiful face and tumors bulged on her bald head, replacing her golden hair. It was clear that she was dying. I wanted to see my friend so my sister and I went to the house. When her mother came to the door, she began to explain the reason for the "no visitors" request. Betty recognized our voices and said, "Let them in." We got to visit, but I cannot remember saying much at all. I was proud and honored to be allowed to make that final visit. She was a dear, brave girl.

Janet Ostergard silently won my heart. Her courage inspired me when we were in the fourth grade. It was book report day and each student was required to go the front of the class and give an oral report on their assigned reading. Our teacher, Miss Callahan, was a tall, thin, silver-brown haired school marm. (A "marm" is the kind of teacher that no child can imagine doing any natural or ordinary things.) She was a sterile kind of being—stiff-backed, with never a hair out of place. Sometimes she smiled.

It is a sunny, warm day when Miss Callahan calls on Janet to give her book report on the Princess and the Pea. Janet quietly asks permission to go to the girl's room, which we call the 'basement' because many of Worcester's old schools put the toilets in the lowest level of the building. However, Roosevelt School is all on one level and the toilets are on each side of the building by the rear doors. Miss Callahan speaks firmly.

"No. You must give your report first."

It is a stern answer and Janet comes to the front of the room and proceeds to give her report. As she speaks, she pees. The puddle gets bigger and bigger. By the end of the report, the stream comes down the aisle between the desks. Janet turns, leaves the classroom and goes home. My heart pounds, I break out in a sweat, and can barely restrain myself from shouting, 'hooray!' Janet is my heroine.

***

HOORAY FOR BULLFROGS!

Most children remember a time when they were not chosen for a game. It always left me feeling "not as good as" and "less than" the best. Selecting the best runners or batters would always leave some child watching from the sidelines. I first believed I could be a member as well as a player in the social world, in junior high. My sister tried out for field hockey and made the team. I tried, but did not qualify. It was not a defeat. Just trying was a positive experience for me and I felt very proud of my sister. At Grafton Street Junior High School, selection for sports was based on skill, but elections for class officers were based on popularity. It was exciting and fun being a part of the election process even though it did not occur to me to run for office. Life began to make sense. (Six years later, in nursing school, I did not hesitate to run for office.)

My greatest enjoyment was socializing with classmates. On our one-hour lunch recess, I walked with, ate with, and visited homes with classmates who lived near the school. Sometimes we simply walked around the neighborhood, popping into shops and saying hello to classmates' parents who worked there. Bus students such as myself carried bag lunches and usually ate in the school cafeteria. Often I had to carry my sandwich as we ventured, because I ate slowly. Traveling in small groups made every adventure more daring and collectivism lent extra delight. As a group, we harassed the mean nuns who would deliberately crowd us off the sidewalk into the street as they led the Parochial School children's squad onto the walkway. I would balance precariously on the edge of the curb until a nun brush-bumped me off the sidewalk. They never looked at me, but used the full-skirted habit with its dangling, heavy wooden cross to fill all the space on the walkway. It was fun, and going with Willie Bourget to his father's jewelry store or with Franny Charbonneau to his dad's cobbler shop, was even more delightful.

The Police Station was in Grafton Square in those days, and waving to officers in Precinct Five was a simple act of friendliness. Policemen were not bothered by our antics and my Grampa had police officer friends, like the Grangers. Going with Katzy Nejaimy to her grandmother's flat was the best of all noontime adventures. Her grandmother cooked bits of tender lamb on a skewer; holding the rod by its tips and gingerly twisting the meat as it roasted over the open flame of the gas stove. Toni Giabatti was the fastest runner on Grafton Hill and just trying to keep up with her was a thrilling lunchtime adventure.

Some of the boys played a card-toss game near the school building. They selected teams by circling in a group, thrusting their fingers into the center as they shouted a number in Italian. Before the toss of the digits there was a declaration of who would begin or be chosen—the odd or the even sum of the total finger count.

"Uno! Duo. . . !" A selection was made and the odd man won.

Excitement, animation and passion wove through every activity at Grafton Street Junior High. On a rainy day, students were allowed to stroll around the box-shaped building with its block-long corridors. We formed two squads, each strolling in opposite directions. You would get to see everybody in one lunch hour. I felt completely alive and included in those three years at Grafton Street Junior High. It was a refreshing contrast to the elementary school game selection methods.

At Roosevelt Grammar School, the game of Blue Bird was supervised by a teacher; a student who selected you, tapped you on your shoulders. Every player sang a ditty while the person who was 'it' wove in and out between people in the circle who were holding their hands up high enough for the "it" person to walk under.

Bluebird, bluebird, through my window,
Bluebird, bluebird, through my window
Bluebird, bluebird, through my window,
Oh Johnny I'm tiiir-ed.
Take a little girl and tap her on her shoulders,
Take a little girl and tap her on her shoulders
Take a little girl and tap her on her shoulders,
Oh Johnny, I'm tiiir-ed.

The child who was tapped on the shoulders became "it" and wove around the circle, making the next selection. Going quickly or slowly would bring you to the classmate you really wanted to choose. Selection was a subtle process of snubbing and elimination.

For teams, the "puh-day-da" (potato) method got you in or out. Everyone in the group put out both hands, held in closed fists. The game leader placed one fist behind his back and used the other to touch each prospective player's fist.

"One puh-day-da, two puh-day-da, three puh-day-da, **four**, five puh-day-da, six puh-day-da, seven puh-day-da, **more**!" The fist touched on **more** had to be placed behind your back. If your other fist was touched on **more,** you were eliminated.

In junior high, I never heard the "N" word, even if the selection process was like grade school, where the finger was pointed at each prospective player waiting to be "popped out." *Eeny, meeny, miney, moe, Catch a bullfrog by the toe—*
If he hollers let him go, Out pops why-oh-you!"

CHAPTER 11

Schoolgirl's Lament

In search of black self, already found
The girl looks black but feels neither black or white
She hears lies about who she really is.
Why can't they see who she is?
"You? You are Africa's child!
Why can't you be content and mild?
We all can see, so why can't you,
that all your folks of the same hue,
came here to *my* land in the bowels of ships
with nappy heads, coal black skin and bulging lips.
Why look and long for a true homeland?
Of course, I know *my* forebears touched the sands
from Europe's shores through immigration gates,
and others have come on boats of late,
as dissidents and political escapees.
For them, the entrance is still not full of ease—
Quiet, girl! You bring confusion and stir up guilt.
So be quiet!"

The black girl rails and the black girl cries.
"Stop! stop right now. Enough of your lies!
Many people came before yours to a land still virgin,
by tribes, they created great nations.
They too had to come from lands afar, centuries ago.

If only you cared to ask, to read, to truly know.
I *know* from whence I came.
My Grandparents from afar, they came here
from Guinea, Bermuda, and Madagascar.
Hush, pitiful pale ones, learn now before it's too late,
we are all one people, one human race;
no one need open any gate.
The planet we share is not owned by you.
It never was nor will it ever be,
and *that's* what's really true!"

—Shirley F. B. Carter (9-5-93)

An angry poem inspired by my Aunt Anna at age 95. She was telling us about her disappointment in finding out that her grandmother was not a Native American, but a Madagascar Indian. She related her story of pain suffered in parochial school, wanting to be absent or ill when the Geography lesson was on Africa—and all her classmates turned and stared at her! She was excluded from the circle game, when classmates refused to touch her brown hands. Her experience paralleled mine and later was confirmed again as an experience of my daughter who sat at Anna's feet. Sadly, I may hear it again from the children of my children. The sting of embarrassment thrust upon defenseless children hurts deeply. The humiliation of exclusion and the taunting of name-calling pierce a child's soul! It was not in my life's plan to have children, because my own childhood was amazing enough and quite daunting. No indeed, raising children was never part of my plans. *I* had survived childhood and that was enough for me.

PART TWO

Learning About Life

CHAPTER 12

Working for Others

1946 to 1949 were my high school years. I worked after school doing childcare. The first year I took care of one child, then the new baby and—on occasion—their cousins too. I worked at the Victory Beauty Salon on weekends. One of my responsibilities was caring for the owner's daughter Penny, who was not in the shop often, but I enjoyed looking out for her. My regular duties were making liquid shampoo from solid globs of green jellied soap, removing hairpins from customers after they came out from under the dryers, sweeping the floors, polishing the furniture and running errands to David's Delicatessen. Customers spent hours at the beauty shop and sent out for food. It was a splendid opportunity to earn tips. I met interesting people and was paid well. I called myself Girl Friday. The last year of High School, I sought additional work. My sister and I needed tuition money for nurses' training. We found short-term jobs such as cleaning test tubes in a laboratory, washing dishes for special events in the Eska Cafeteria and working for a dentist, Dr. Marshall.

***

LULLS

Sometimes life just seemed to pause when work was not an issue: sparkling pauses such as those we experienced when we went to the Esplanade on Storrow Drive by Boston's Charles River. The Boston Pops played there and the concerts were free. I was—and still am—connected to music in wonderful ways. I saw pictures in my mind. It was not as it was at Bobby Birtz's house, when we listened to the William Tell overture and became the Lone Ranger. Bouncing on the couch in a yippie-aye-ky-yea way held its own special delight, but that was kid stuff. This was more subdued. I was now a young adult lying on the grass, just peering up at the sky and allowing the music to take me away. Each instrument conjured up an image in my mind. The tuba was the greatest! Humungous gray elephants lumbered into view, swaying their trunks and lolling their great heads in perfect harmony. Flute sounds called up little fluttering birds as well as gliding birds: hawks and eagles floating on thermals to rest at great heights or swooping to seize their prey. It was fabulous, visualizing the marvels the sounds paraded forth.

"Oh Audrey, here come the elephants again."

My sister, more befuddled than disturbed, gave me that *what's wrong with you now?* look.

"The music, the tuba! Can't you just see the elephants?" This made Audrey curious. She propped up on one elbow and glanced at her excited sister.

"What *are* you talking about?"

It never occurred to me that not everyone could see an image while listening to music. Classical music and the Boston Pops programs were especially good at conjuring up great pictures. With patience, I explained:

"You know, like when you look up there and see the clouds rolling and making shapes—like ships, or big bears, all kinds of reminders of things. You know, like that. Now, *LISTEN*. Hear the flute. Taa-daa, twit-a-twit, twit-diddle, diddle, a-twit-twit! A twit-a-twit, a twit-diddle, diddle, a-twit-a-twit! It's a bird, scampering across the sand. See it? Can't you *see* it?"

My sister's face looked blank, then reflected something close to pity. The staccato trumpets sent the seabirds into hurried flight in my mind. Then it happened: the tubas started up and I sounded off:

"Baaa-rump, ba-rump, baaa-rump, ba-rump, Barump-arumpedy, ump-dy, dump!" The slow deep tones were pure pachyderm! Audrey rolled her eyes at me.

"Close your eyes!" I demanded. "Now *look* while you listen. See them? See the elephants?"

I could see them with my eyes wide open, but the tubas made their best magic with eyes shut.

"Oh my, oh yah." A tiny smile tried to wrinkle Audrey's cupid lips as she allowed an elephant image to lumber into the recesses of her imagination—this *imagination place*, where her harsh life experiences had never before allowed her to venture. It became a special treat to share imaginary places with my sister. Audrey became my soul buddy, the person I could look at from across a room and with whom I could silently share a common vision.

CHAPTE13

Saints

When they were children, my mother and her sisters attended All Saints Church in Worcester, shortly after their arrival from Malden. Mom would say with pride, "Some of my pennies rebuilt this church after the fire. All of us children pitched in our pennies."

All Saints Church had had two devastating fires: in 1874 the building on Pearl Street burned to the ground. The new building was raised on Irving Street where it stands today. It took many years to construct all the previous buildings. The second fire in 1932 was not so destructive. Her life had been simpler then and she would sometimes share some pleasant memories of All Saints with us.

In *my* youth, church was both a haven and an oppressive institution. What made it a haven for me was my childlike acceptance of God as Father of all. I was very young and passionate, and with Jesus as my brother and God as my father, I could hold out hope for myself and for the rest of the world. My father, who was Roman Catholic, had seen to it that Audrey, his first-born, was baptized in the Catholic Church. That had happened in Cambridge; we moved to Sharon and then to Worcester. I was baptized at All Saints after my parents became members. The Great Depression of the

'30s made life difficult everywhere. The Barrow family could not pledge a specific amount to the church. Poverty prevailed. After my father left us, the resulting divorce became an additional issue with the church.

My baptism was special and awesome. I was intimidated by the experience because, unlike the others at the ceremony, I was not a baby—I was five years old. I walked down the long aisle to the font wearing my best clothes, my Sunday shoes clacking loudly on the shiny, marble floor. The ritual was repetitive, mesmerizing and scary. The holy water ran down my forehead to my lips. It tasted salty, and I suspect that, although I didn't cry like the babies, a tear must have snuck down my cheek.

Church was serious, solemn and truly mystical for me. Each Sunday I watched the choir process in cadence down the same aisle. The men's voices were so loud and powerful that my entrails literally shook within me.

One of the most thrilling choral events at All Saints was the Easter pageant. The men became Roman soldiers in full regalia: mail, swords, helmets and all! The organ music filled the church and proclaimed the miracle of the risen Christ. The men sang the story about the body being stolen, then the Sunday school children returned with:

Fie old Roman, why tell a lie, fie old Roman, why tell a lie, for Christ is risen, Christ is risen indeed. Alleluia, amen!

I sang the melody as loud as I could with defiant jubilation!

A cross-shaped, hollow box stood tall near the steps to the altar, resembling an empty coffin designed to hold the many Sunday School mite-boxes. We paraded to the cross, filling it with our boxes bundled in cloth bags closed with drawstrings. Bright red geraniums decked the steps to the altar and their pungent smell with the intoxicating aroma of sweet lilies and hyacinths, combined to make the miracle as real as life itself. My spirit soared to an ethereal place away from cold, hunger or any sadness.

The annual church school picnic was at Lake Park, and my Brownie Troop was part of the magic of All Saints for me. This picnic was for all the Episcopal churches in the city and crowds of children rode trolley cars to the park. It was great fun hanging onto overhead hand loops, delightedly swaying and rocking all the way to Lake Quinsigamond.

The Girl Scout Brownie Troop leaders, Miss Monigal and Miss Beers, were shining examples of saints to me. One of our hymns stated it clearly: ordinary people could be saints and, as this hymn declared, *"I want to be one too."* These women welcomed the troop into their home. We made Waldorf salad with apples and nuts, carrots and sweet raisins. Brownies wore uniforms and these women managed to find one to fit me as my family did not have money to buy one. My uniform wasn't quite the same shade of brown as the other girls.'

Sundays at All Saints remained a welcoming time and place for me even though my mother was no longer welcome as she was a divorced person and therefore could not pledge. She maligned the priest and his unchristian attitude, dubbing him, "Richard Greedy," but set aside twenty cents for bus and trolley fare for Audrey and me. That gave me a few more years at this haven. I put one dime in the collection plate and walked the four miles home from church.

The goodness I saw in people always made them seem saintly. Men in particular, were either absent, despised or sainted. My grandfather was one of my first earthly saints and Dr. Marshall, a black dentist, also qualified for sainthood. Audrey and I worked for him in our teenage years to earn tuition money for nursing school. He worked on our teeth, using painless, advanced techniques. My porcelain fillings were nearly invisible and lasted for years.

War bonds from my aunt Anna, along with our savings from multiple jobs was not enough for the required tuition. My neighbor, Dotty, had a boyfriend—Jimmy—who thumbed his way from college in Syracuse, New York, across the country and gave his flight money to my sister and myself so that we could have the full amount in time to enter nurses' training. Dotty married him after he graduated from college. He later entered the ministry and then became a teacher. Such acts of love reinforced my belief that there were saints on earth.

My friend Gordon also confirmed my belief in goodness and in the existence of pure love. He attended All Saints Church. As a young adult, I belonged to another parish and the young adults from the two churches shared events. I met Gordon there. It was an active, adventuresome group, and when we became too old to belong to that group, Gordon and I maintained a friendship. We went to flower shows and to church social events and shared quiet, thoughtful times together. We loved the ceremony of the church, the beauty of the earth and each other. It was a platonic love that never suffered any misunderstanding or loss. Eventually I moved away, wrote one long love letter and got to spend precious time with him at the very end of his life in April of 1987. A grave illness took him away, yet I never lost his gift of unselfish love. Church allowed me to reach for the places where spirits dwell, and the saints I was introduced to taught me about redemption and grace.

CHAPTER 14

The Other Side of the Tracks

To get to Summer Street, we walked from Irving Street down Pleasant Street, across Main Street to Central Street. From Main Street, many streets like Thomas, Central and Exchange connected to Summer Street. They all crossed over the railroad tracks and into another world, and there I came upon Laurel, Clayton and Carol Streets, where my aunts lived. This was a place where everything and everybody seemed warm, unhurried—and colored. Sweet sounds melted from velvet-voiced horns that called to each other when the sun slid down to rest and folks moved out to their stoops and porches and into the alleyways. On the summer breeze, the yeasty smell of Bond Bread floated past the flats and cottages. There were also several small shops, a tobacco store with penny-candy and a Chinese laundry.

Usually on Sunday, right after church, my whole family would arrive at Aunt Elsie's flat. Elsie's place was different. She'd be sitting in her curtain-less window, resting her chocolate arms on the sill and greeting people as they ambled up the little hill. She played cards a lot and ate pickled pig's feet. Her hair was short, her smile was quick and she always seemed happy to see us. Dinner was in the making; the kind of dinner with hot biscuits and gravy, served with mushy vegetables boiled in broth or smothered in a big black spider—a frying pan—with pork. It tasted wonderful! In the back room where it was cool, the cloth-covered desserts were huddled: pudding made from scratch with cornstarch, whole milk, eggs, vanilla, rich dark chocolate and scorched brown-sugary butterscotch. The pudding would form a thick rubbery lid as it cooled down and I would slip my finger under the lid to get a taste before dinner. There was always a feeling of "forbidden" that went along with the joy of being at Elsie's house. I got to play in the street and run through the whole neighborhood with my Hampton cousins. My cousins used to say I lived "out in the country" and somehow that wasn't the place where people who looked like me lived. They all lived on the East Side or the West Side.

"None of that kind of talk here!" My mother would rant and rave at us if we said "dese," "doze" or "dat."

"What's wrong with 'dat?'" I can't hear anything wrong in the way people talk. Some people say, "ask" and other people say, "ax.' " What is so bad about words?

Then the ominous lecture would begin. It was so confusing to me. Why would some people not amount to anything because of the way they talked? Why would living on the other side of the tracks destine you to a hard life? Nothing my mother said could convince me that I was lucky not to live on the "other side of the tracks." What *did* cause me to consider my good fortune was the scary dance the roaches did if I had to put the light on at night to go in the toilet or peeked into the room where the boys slept. The beds were broken and they slept on mattresses without sheets. We didn't stay overnight much at Elsie's and by the time I was in the sixth grade we didn't see my cousins much at all. None of us attended All Saint's Church any more. Our after-church ritual was broken.

Cousin Joyce was the girl cousin closest to my age. It was Joyce who grabbed our hands and ran, terrified, away from the Community Center on Laurel Street when my dad came out of the Center towards us. My father worked there, and it was clear to adults and to young girls like Joyce, that my mother and father were battling. Joyce took his action as a threat.

"Is he going to steal us from our mom?"

He had tried to do so once before. We were walking in front of my mother down Exchange Street when he suddenly appeared and reached for me. Audrey noticed, and screeched with such force she broke a blood vessel in her forehead. She remembers the black and blue mark that remained long after the incident.

This Sunday when we were with cousin Joyce, he didn't have a chance. Joyce ran our legs to jelly until we reached the safety of her house where my mother was visiting her sister, Elsie—Joyce's mom. Joyce was commended for her action.

The adults' reaction was quite different with cousin Richard. One day he was out in the country at our house when he proposed a game. The girls were supposed to drop their pants and bend over, and then it would be Richard's turn to do the same thing. I saw my mother through the kitchen window making something for us all to eat. I waved to her just as the game began. Her eyes got big, her face wrinkled up so much that she looked ugly and unreal and I could see her mouth shaped in a screech as she leaned toward the window and began banging on it. She looked like she was going to fly right through it. I couldn't move. She often told us not to make ugly faces.

"Would you like your face to freeze like that?" she would ask. At that moment her face was the most horrifying thing I had ever seen. If it froze like that, I wouldn't know who she was! She got out of the door faster than I could imagine her coming through the window, screaming at Richard. He ran off crying; he cried *before* they caught him and whipped him seemingly forever.

***

In spite of that incident, Richard was one of my favorite cousins. After we grew up, his banter, lively intellect and imagination blossomed. He always made me aware of the affection he held for me. He had been treated badly by adults. Grown-ups talked about the way he was neglected as an infant. He'd been left for so many hours or even days in wet diapers that he had suffered severe pelvic burns. My grandmother supposedly healed his wounds with sulfa and lard.

***

Whenever Richard and I got together, we'd talk for hours. He'd make believe he was speaking a foreign language, then would talk seriously about the world, switch gears and explain his notion about the Age of Aquarius. He was wise before his time.

Richard rescued me down south. When he was in

the Air force in 1957, he came to visit me in Washington DC and we went for a drive. There were three of us in my car: Oscar Carter, my husband—who we called O.D.—Richard and myself. I was driving. We were rear-ended as I signaled to make a left turn and slowed down. The fender buckled into the left rear tire and I wasn't sure I could drive it. The two young men who were driving the other car and I were exchanging information when I discovered that not only was their car unregistered, but neither of them had a driving license with them.

"*Neither* of you have a driver's license? Who does the car belong to?" I gave a sigh of relief when I saw the police coming. I was copying their car's plate number when the officer announced he was placing, O.D., Richard and myself under arrest. I began to argue loudly. There were no other cars in the intersection and no one even stopped to see what was going on.

"I demand to know what you are charging us with!"

O.D. implored me to be quiet. Richard was silent and aghast while O.D. stooped down and pulled the fender far enough away from the tire so he could drive if we went straight ahead. We were escorted to the Police Station to be booked. I could not keep quiet.

"I demand to know why we are under arrest! What's the charge? I know I have a right to a phone call!"

An officer behind a high wooden counter drawled out, "Let huh make huh damn phone cawll an' shut huh up." I called the Automobile Legal Aid emergency number listed on the back of my membership card.

"What precinct are you in? How much is the fine?"

I was calmed by the responder's gentle tone, and asked the officer for the information. The desk officer slowly and deliberately gave me the precinct name and number and recited the charge.

". . . obstruction uh traffic. That's uh fifty dollah faahn."

The ALA agent metered out a slow, deliberate response.

"Pay the fifty dollars and get out of there now. We will reimburse your fine. Do you understand me, Ma'am? Pay and get out of there."

His serious, deliberate tone riveted me and caused me to catch my breath. O.D. and I did not have fifty dollars. My panicked gaze met Richard's whose usually dreamy, smiling eyes were open wide. He moved forward as though he was stepping out of rank, pulled the money out of his pocket and handed it to the officer. The men were silent. In a sweeping move, Richard put his arm around me and ushered me out the door.

"I want a receipt!" My feeble, parting protest annoyed O.D.

"For God's sake shut up!"

My legs were trembling and I began to weep. The baby inside me wiggled and jiggled and kicked and I shook and wept all the way home. Richard was my hero that day. He died in April of 1982 of liver disease and multiple degenerative maladies associated with a hard life. All but one of my Hampton cousins are dead. I am convinced that life was harder on them, living on the other side of the tracks. Those damned tracks signified more than I could ever imagine. I grew up speaking proper English and longing to know people who looked like me, and I thank God for my cousins.

PART THREE

Making My Way

CHAPTER 15

Resolution

"What's the resolution?" My sister Anita was visiting and I told her I was writing my memoir. She asked to read it but couldn't finish reading the draft. "There's so much sadness; so many problems. Have you thought about history; considered telling about what was going on in the world?"

I did not plan to focus on the world events in the time when I was growing up. History has already been selectively recorded. Wars, the depression and the civil rights movement were significant events in my life and—of course—my experience of them was affected by my color. Our father was a member of an all-black regiment that was not allowed to serve with white soldiers. His unit was sent overseas and fought side by side with the French and other European troops. He wore pins on his uniform presented by the French military in recognition of the valorous deeds done by colored troops. When President Harry Truman integrated the armed services, my father was greatly disappointed, disheartened and angry. He was certain he would never again enjoy the pride and *esprit de corps* of men like himself. He also believed that—as an officer—he could never be up front leading his troops without wondering when and if some disgruntled "cracker" would "accidentally" shoot him in the back.

The depression affected everyone in the late nineteen-twenties and early nineteen-thirties, but for my family, the depression did not end. It was well into the nineteen-fifties, and long after the pre- and postwar economic booms before my family could pool enough of their resources to get water and electricity on Ellen Street. The City's utility departments felt it wasn't cost-effective to run water pipes and electric lines up a street for the only two families on it who had no water or electricity. There were three other families on Ellen Street. Their utility connections came from Grafton Street or Margin Street. We were the only black families on the street and in that part of town—and I am certain that was part of the city's indifference.

Redcaps, Pullman Porters, maids and elevator operators earned substandard wages and these were the only jobs available to colored people.

Throughout the nineteen sixties, my daughters and I watched assassinations, attack dogs, fire-hosings, bombings, sit-ins, marches and murders nightly on television. There was no rational way to explain that kind of racism to children, colored or white. It was simply horrible! But hope, satisfaction and resolve came in the form of small triumphs that happened throughout my life, regardless of the times or the insane hatred, benign neglect and blatant ignorance.

When I was very young, my idea for a career was to have a job like the lovely lady in Denholm's Department store. She looked like me and she maintained the ladies room on the second floor tucked away in the back of the store and up a tiny stairwell. The woman's smooth, brown, smiling face greeted each person warmly. She usually sat in a chair near the entry and welcomed you silently. Probably the tips that generous women left in her basket were the bulk of her salary. My mother never left tips, but always greeted the woman like a friend. From my young viewpoint, it looked like a wonderful job. During my teen years, I yearned for loftier careers, first an aviatrix, then an eye surgeon.

Audrey had decided on her career while still in kindergarten. She planned to become a nurse and to marry John Con, a classmate who decided he was going to be a doctor. I don't know what became of John Con, but Audrey began her practice at age five by cutting my diabetic grandparents' toenails, patiently oiling their feet and tending to their needs. I changed my goals after investigating what was required of me to fly airplanes or operate on eyes. While working at the Victory Beauty Salon, I shared my wish to become an eye surgeon. A generous woman offered to sponsor my surgical training in a school in Scotland, because there I could be admitted to a medical school and color would not be an issue. But the thought of living that far away from home was intolerable.

My mother, her sister Evelyn and other colored women ran the elevators in most of Worcester's department stores and office buildings. As a practical move, I applied to become a licensed elevator operator, passed the tests and offered my mother a summer off while I ran her elevator. I studied, then took the test for my license on a hydraulic elevator. It was in the Day Building at its side entrance on Maple Street. The front of the building faced Main Street, number 306. Many of the interesting people who used the side entrance came to take lessons: elocution, voice and instruments. It was a wonderful, busy, noisy place. The elevator was an open iron-lace cage that allowed me to see every floor as I glided up. It was powered by a monstrous, water-driven plunger that required particular skill when trying to stop level with the floor. Moving the control too quickly caused the cage to bounce violently, forcing my stomach to adjust and requiring several more bounces to match the level of the floor. I was prone to motion sickness; did not intend to bounce my way up and down the floors and quickly became an expert at gliding and leveling. I could slide the heavy iron, diamond-shaped, folding gate doors without making a clatter.

There were no such challenges running the elevator at 34 Mechanic Street. I trained on and worked on the hydraulic elevator until an Inspector could schedule a test. Then I was licensed. Running an electric elevator was simple, the solid doors were modernized and opened automatically but, to work in my mother's building, I needed the license. She had a close working relationship with her boss so it was easily arranged. There were three floors in the building where she worked on Mechanic Street. On the second floor there was a loan finance company and a radio station and on the ground level the elevator opened into a wide, tile-floored hallway. Off the hallway a furniture company was on the left and the Gas Company to the right.

Downstairs was a special place to me. It was once an air raid shelter and was still used to store old wartime equipment that had been used by air wardens. There were red triangles on shelter signs on top of boxes, big lantern-shaped flashlights and white hard-hats. All the generators, fuse boxes and heating equipment were huddled down there in out-of-the-way corners and under huge metal beams. My mother and her coworker, Harry, were a team who knew where every switch and control was located. The owners called upon them in times of emergency as they both knew what to do and whom to call if a system failed. When I was not baby-sitting or doing some other after-school job, I would go to her workplace. She would let me go downstairs and I would wait for her in a little room she shared with Harry. The elevator door opened on to the cellar; a deep, black hole with no windows. It took a while, but I eventually managed to locate the door lock without first searching for the string that hung from the only light at the end of the basement. Once inside the room, the space became insular, cozy. Its many-tiered shelves, cluttered with paper towels, toilet paper and all kinds of building supplies, sheltered and surrounded me. Being there every day for two weeks, the place lost all its charm..

That summer I worked for my mother moved me to a new resolution: I could never spend the rest of my life running an elevator! The boredom I experienced hurt my entire being. This was the summer of 1949 when I decided to be a nurse like my sister was planning to be. It was a wise and wonderful resolution.

CHAPTER 16

Life at Thayer Hall

Before we were admitted to the Worcester City Hospital School of Nursing, there were some doubts expressed by the Director of Nurses, Margaret Dieter, who asked some pointed questions. Her interview with us was direct.

"We've had a few Jews . . . .We do not want to risk losing any fully-paid students if you have to share a room . . . . Perhaps we could try it for six months. You could room together." There were more statements, this time about money.

"We will expect payment in advance to cover the first six months, then there's the breakage fee deposit. You pay for your uniforms of course, and there are tests you must take to see if you are academically suited. Your Intelligence Test scores must be on par and your math—you've only had two years of college math? A review of decimals, percentages and fractions will suffice. Miss Dieter's impersonal dismissal was not upsetting. The requirements were laid out and we had no doubt that we could meet them. We did.

***

The nurses' home, Thayer Hall, was a splendid brick

building on 68 Jaques Avenue, directly across the street from Worcester City Hospital.

It was like a military nunnery. Nursing students had "privileges"—a Sunday off once a month and an hour break during evening study times. There were inspections, room checks, curfews and uniform patdowns. We were expected to wear girdles and carry our scissors in our waistbands. In spite of the harassment and militaristic overtones, the first six months were a great adventure. Contrary to Miss Dieter's concerns about losing white students who would not want to room with black girls, each student had her own room. It was pristine, efficient and perfectly wonderful. For the first time in my life I had my own closet, a desk, a sink, a bureau, and a window that opened onto a flat roof. The room was warm, and the large common bathroom at the end of the hall had rows of showers and modern flush toilets. Some toilets back then still had wooden water boxes above them—with a chain and wooden handle you pulled.

Because students could not cross the lobby in their nightclothes, I pranced across the roof to other classmates' rooms. Mischief and games lightened up the grueling routine that consisted of going on duty at dawn, setting up special diets, loading large stainless steel food carts; washing bed pans, folding linens and filling canisters with precisely folded sponges for autoclaving. These duties had to be completed before we could run to catch the bus to college. I would run across the street, disrobing en route—loosening the black tie, unbuttoning studs that held the starched white bib to the equally starched apron down to the basic blue under-dress, ready to don street clothes.

Even after our morning showers, professors on campus would complain about the smell of sweat that came with the nursing students. I was in constant motion and before the six months ended, I was on night duty.

I worked alone. Many nights I prayed for my aged patients who often died at first light and it was a fierce challenge to get the resident, prepare the body for the morgue and then get off duty in time for school. It was a tough shift and by the end of the semester, almost impossible to stay awake in college. I fell asleep in chemistry class but the professor never embarrassed any of the exhausted students. I was lucky. I loved chemistry; the lab and the campus atmosphere, plus the college text was identical to my high school chemistry book. The nursing students were also required to join a club and participate in student activities. All of us joined the French Club because they met at a time we were on campus and they served refreshments. It was great fun.

We had fun too in the nursing school dormitory and the wards. Janet was assigned to the orthopedic ward where she was asked to set up a sky hook traction for a new admission diagnosed with a fractured hymen. I could laugh along with the jokesters once I found out what a hymen was. Some of the male students were military veterans and many of the nurses in the senior class were military cadets, so teen-aged freshmen were sometimes targets of the veterans' teasing. A prank that I remember involved a male nursing student with an attitude. He bragged about how much more work he could do than the girls could and spouted other nonsense about female weakness. The female student nurses told him that they had some pills that gave them extra energy and offered him some. He took the bait. They'd gotten some urology dye used to test kidney efficiency that made your urine bright blue-green. His horrified howls were heard clearly by the tricksters waiting outside the lavatory.

I learned how to smoke and soon I could blow smoke rings and flip a lighted cigarette safely inside my mouth to avoid being caught but the housemother never caught me. It was too easy—no challenge—so on the next trip to the corner store I bought Baby Ruth candy bars. For the twenty cents the cigarettes cost, I could buy *four* candy bars.

At Thayer Hall there were as many pleasures as there were pranks. The nurse's lounge had a television set. I often joined the rowdy afternoon group who flopped on easy chairs and watched the Mickey Mouse Club, making fun of it while enjoying every minute. Food was especially good at Worcester City Hospital. In the dormitory kitchen there were commercial-sized tins of peanut butter and jelly, along with fresh eggs, bread and butter and gallons of milk. The cafeteria served foods I had never experienced: salads, kielbasa, cabbage-wrapped beef and rice, gooey-crunchy chocolate nut brownie cake, glorified rice with maraschino cherries, pineapple and whipped cream. My mother cooked chicken, pork roasts, fish, hamburgers and hot dogs and that was all. Even at night the orderly brought the nurses sandwiches and bad-tasting coffee. I enjoyed it all.

Working on the orthopedic ward, I had another unique experience with food—homemade food. Unlike the female nurses, male nurses could be married, and they all lived off campus in apartments paid for by the

City. Harold worked the ward with me. He showed off his culinary expertise by bringing in pots of food on the evening shift. His nickname was "the Dragon." He made great spaghetti, but one day he used red-hot peppers in the sauce. It made my mouth sing and cry out for milk or anything that would put out the fire. It was an even greater shock to discover that hot peppers react painfully to all mucous tissue, both on the way down and on the way out! The Dragon was one fiery cook.

After three years at Thayer Hall, I was no longer a thin, shy, dark colored girl. I was a well groomed, one hundred and fifty-pound confident woman, ready to embrace the world. At the age of twenty, this pale colored girl had become a skilled, professional, trained nurse.

CHAPTER 17

Where Confidence Comes From

For graduates of three-year hospital nursing training programs, there is no mystery about the genesis of nursing confidence. I hope my story will remind the maturing diploma school graduates of their own wonderful tales.

The usual student rotation in the 1940s and 1950s at Worcester City Hospital School of Nursing was from medical to surgical wards. Specialties such as pediatrics, and surgery followed, then obstetrics. I was an eager, bright-eyed, first-year nursing student placed in error in an early rotation to obstetrics.

On the first day of my obstetric rotation I was ushered into the delivery room to assist with a birth, never expecting to see the miracle that unfolded in front of my eyes. At eighteen years of age I knew a little about a few things and almost nothing about human sexuality, the birth of babies, or the female anatomy.

The mother was on an awful looking table with her knees bent and legs in stirrups. The drapes hid her face from view. Dr. S, a well-known and well-respected obstetrician, was performing the delivery. I stared at the bulging, shaved perineum.

"She's crowning. Good," said Dr. S.

Dr. S. seemed to talk to himself a lot, then encouraged the face behind the lump of draped knees. He never looked towards me or the small stainless steel table on wheels that rested beside me.

"Kelley!...Kelley!" he yelled.

I didn't know who the masked, gowned circulating nurse who scooted me into that small room was, but Kelley never came. The baby's hair looked like it was matted with white petroleum jelley. Its tiny face popped from the bulging vulva, then shoulders, two arms, and heavens above, a whole howling baby was in his hands. I'd never seen anything like it in my life.

"Kelley! Kelley! He said in an angry voice. He turned, narrowed his eyes to slits, and scowled at me. "Get her out of here!"

He called another name. The masked mystery nurse flew into the room and slapped instruments into his hand and wheeled the waiting isolette to his side.

I never saw who Kelley was, but I couldn't stop smiling at the miracle I had witnessed. This was going to be a wonderful rotation!

Later on, it was discovered that I had never done my surgical rotation. No time was wasted getting me up to to speed. I learned how to listen to fetal heart rates, souffles (soft blowing sounds heard on oscultation) maternal heart rates,...and the names of instruments such as "kelley."

Towards the end of my obstetric rotation, I was assigned to a mother who was medically compromised. Her infant was hydrocephalic and was vaginally undeliverable. The mother was exhausted and surgery was iminent. I carefully monitored the fetal heart rate, and the mother's vital signs. My shift ended just as the cluster of consulting obstetricians decided the mother's life was at such risk they would attempt to reduce the size of the newborn baby's head using a trocar and cannula to drain off fluid from the skull. The baby was to be sacrificed to save the mother. I got permission to stay on duty and "special" the mother, whom I'd suported all shift. I continued to take and chart the fetal heart rate and the mother's vital signs.

"Don't take any more fetal rates. The baby is dead," instructed the supervisor.

The mother was still alert enough to hear the conversations about her peril and the decision to sacrifice the baby to save her. I continued to record the heart rate.

Don't chart that. It's just the souffle you're hearing."

But I had learned so much during this rotation, and I knew what I was hearing. The mother's pulse was slow, her condition was grave. The fetal heart and souffle were rapid. The supervisor questioned my credibility, and the physician ignored my charting, but this mother and unborn child had become my "project." The patient was rushed to surgery, and I wanted to see her through it. My supervisor told me I couldn't go. I pleaded and finally got permission to stand in the amphitheater.

The procedure had already started when I scrambled to my viewing spot. The OR souepvisor gave me a nervous glance. Dr. S. Never looked up. He called for a specimen plate, placed the baby on it, and called for sutures. The baby's face had a gaping space where his upper lip should be and his mouth opened right into his nose. And then he howled!

The OR suddenly looked like an old-fashioned movie, with people quickly scurrying and shouting.

"Suction! Somebody get that suction!"

"Get an incubator!"

I stood in the balcony and smiled. The mother and her baby survived, and a young student nurse discovered where confidence comes from.

CHAPTER 18

Her Place

They wanted to come to my house, these women in nurses' training who were like sisters. We sang together in the evening, studied together at night. We strolled through the neighborhood, trying to wake up, trying to revive our brains so we could retain more and more information. We cried together and pleaded with each other not to give up.

"The door swings both ways . . ." was the mantra the nursing instructors repeated to remind us that our presence was always conditional. Nurses' training was intense. Life, death, closeness and difference blended in this unusual environment. We ate together, lived in separate rooms yet were no longer strangers from different worlds. I knew they liked me, but they had no clue to what my life was like outside Thayer Hall Dormitory even though they knew my sister and my mother. My heart sank in fear of being found out. If they came to my house they'd know the awful truth. They'd discover the ugly reality of how I grew up.

"I'll meet you in the TV room," Sully reminded me.

"OK," I said, preparing myself to accept the inevitable. The four of us would hop on the number five bus, then ride almost to the end of the line. My house was a lot nearer than Sully's house—*her* bus took us out of Worcester, left us off at a stone wall just past an abandoned motel on the highway. That's where we looked for the horse. Whichever child came home first would ride the horse to the house, then send her back down pasture to graze near the stone wall. All of us piled on the old mare and swayed up the hill to the Sullivan's house. I had visited there at least once.

The number five bus meandered across town making multiple stops. Bus transportation was popular in the 1940's. My mind wandered.

Will this be it? When they see the one room, the oil lamps . . . ? If they have to go to the bathroom . . . ? They believe that they are not prejudiced, but I know better. Late-night discussions about race disclosed their buried feelings. They had been tainted by a racist society. They don't believe it, but it comes out, as it always does.

"In Webster we don't have any colored people," *Eloise explains.*

"What makes you think you are not prejudiced?" I ask.

"Well, well . . . just never was." Eloise is certain. "It's nineteen forty-nine, prejudice is history." She is so confident.

The entire student body of the Worcester City Hospital School of Nursing confirmed Eloise's position. Young people are not born prejudiced; asked their opinion when they trust their own thinking, they demonstrate their non-racist beliefs. That had already happened, but I remembered how that late night discussion had ended.

"So you really believe that racism hasn't affected you?" I wanted to inject some reality into this naïve, small town perspective. Others chimed in to confirm that they too were sure they had not been influenced by society's scourge.

I put them to the ultimate test. "What if my son wanted to marry your daughter?"

"Oh no! That wouldn't be right," they all agreed.

"That would never happen" they concluded and went quickly on to another subject. I knew they had all been influenced by society. Now, how would they deal with the reality of poverty?

To my great surprise, they were charmed! With honest exuberance, they were enchanted by lamplight. My father, then Captain Barrow, had left us to live in an unfinished house with no glass in the upstairs windows, no electricity, no running water and a cast-iron stove with no fuel. Tarpaper closed off one large space for us to live in and warded off the wind, rain and snow. Mother shoveled snow from upstairs to keep it from melting, leaking down and soaking our beds. She made flannel sacks to hold bricks that were kept warm on the back of the black stove by day, and were tucked into our beds at night to keep our feet from freezing. For many years we lugged water, dug new pits for the outhouse and carried gallons of kerosene to keep the converted wood stove working. We three women had passed a severe survival test but I felt no sense of pride in our accomplishment. It was incredible to me that my classmates went to the outhouse uttering no complaint or negative comment. They were curious, complimentary and maintained our friendship without reservation after the visit.

I had never received such acceptance from adults. Even the most well intentioned grown-ups had crushed my spirit with some betraying act of ugly, irrational,

Miss Scully

racist behavior. One particular example of this prejudice was the nursing arts instructor, Kathryn Scully, who I viewed as my modern-day Florence Nightingale. Miss Scully seemed to tower in her white uniform. More thin and erect than tall, her carriage exuded sterility and starch. Her pale skin was not saggy; wrinkled perhaps, but she did not look terribly old—just a wee bit embalmed, resembling a placid, bisque doll. We dedicated our yearbook to Miss Scully. She was an exemplary professional nurse. I realized the importance of not expecting every white person to act overtly racist. I could not live and thrive in a world where everyone would hate me on sight, so I thought it was safe to assume that Miss Scully liked me. I was a good student and excelled in nursing arts.

It was after the six-month probationary period. Audrey and I had both passed all our studies and received our coveted caps. City Hospital nursing students were required to attend Worcester State College for all of our sciences, history, social studies, and physical education. My marks were just fine and both of our nursing skills were in the top rank. The six-month probationary period had flown by and the capping ceremony had confirmed our success.

The day Miss Scully called us to her office I was proudly wearing my new cap, starched bib and wristwatch. (Probationers—"Probies"—had to wear their watches around their necks, suspended on a strand of black grosgrain ribbon.) Miss Scully addressed us. What now, I wondered?

"There is something I want to tell you." Miss Scully's nun-like composure complemented her sparsely decorated office and offered no clue for the reason for the summons. She sat behind her desk.

"I honestly never expected you girls would make it through the probationary period. I regret my vote." She must have seen the confusion in our eyes. "Yes, there was a vote before you girls were admitted to the School. The City Council approved it and then it was up to the faculty and the student body. I voted not to admit you, just as the rest of the faculty members did. Surprisingly, the student body voted to admit—a one hundred-percent vote. Well, since they would be the ones who would have to live with you and since they were so willing, you were admitted." She paused. "I feared the uniform would be somewhat degraded . . . ." Her voice droned on.

My body felt on fire. My stomach shifted into reverse. If the meeting had gone on a moment longer, I knew I would vomit! My head reeled, hearing Miss Scully's matter-of-fact, pitiless tone just lay it out—*she and the entire faculty voted no!* It was like seeing someone naked, noticing for the first time how strangely designed and weird they really were. Why didn't she keep herself covered? Why did she in essence disrobe and expose her ugly prejudice right in front of me? Was she trying to apologize? From that moment on, I knew my place as far as Miss Scully and the other faculty members were concerned.

CHAPTER 19

Green Monkey

Ma wrung her hands, shook her head and muttered, "I hate that thing. Damn green monkey!"

It sat there, shining. Its fired, ceramic green surface reflected light. It was one of my favorite souvenirs. Like the Bavarian beer steins, it was made to hold alcoholic beverages and, when lifted to pour, its Swiss music element chimed beautiful melodies. I loved that monkey; to me it symbolized emancipation. That green monkey had come from Germany where I had gone on invitation to visit with my father and had the opportunity to buy things to bring home.

"Gonna find out things, gonna take this guy up on the offer."

This was the man whom I could not call father, who we had nicknamed Black Beard—the villain. This was the same man who, in my mind, I'd killed off when I was very young.

People would ask, "Where is your father?"

"My father?" I would say, "He's dead."

"What happened?"

"Oh—the army. He was in the army."

This was the only explanation I could give curious people. How could any man just disappear and abandon his children and his wife? But Herbert was more com-

plex than his four-year-old daughter could imagine, and now I was twenty-one and still did not understand the man.

To Dorothy the monkey was the symbol of horror—a horrible time, a horrible event, a terrible happening; a loss she could not get over, when her daughter had left her to go to Germany. Dorothy had lost her dutiful little girl who would give her attention at any time and pull her up out of her well of despair far enough to cope with the world. Her harsh existence appeared more manageable when it was viewed through a loving child's eyes.

I was a bit like Pollyanna, growing up in a house of utter deprivation. If only the monkey could talk to her. Then she'd understand what going to Germany was all about.

Ma could talk—she told and retold her life story whenever she was melancholy. She acted as if she was losing the last of her children when Audrey and I went to Germany. Throughout her life she had experienced many losses and so shrouded herself in sadness, adorning herself in its darkness as if it were a mink stole.

"I lost my father when I was a girl—no, no, he didn't die," she'd lament. "When I was the youngest I was his companion. He brought me everywhere." There were pictures of her as a child in starched pinafores with ribbons in her hair, gazing at the camera with dreamy, soulful eyes.

I thought my mother Dorothy was beautiful. Her description of her life, her home and her dog made me feel envious. After all she had a father, she grew up in a nice house, and had two generous parents who still lived next door—right on Ellen Street!

Change and the loss of her father's undivided attention had come for Dorothy in 1912 when what she expected to be a blessed event—little sister Evelyn—came into the world: the family then left Malden to come to Worcester, where her father found better work. He was the horticulturist who had proudly showed and taught his employers and assistant helpers the hows and whys of successful cultivation. They followed his instruction, learned his skills and then let him go.

Dreadful things seemed to have happened to Dorothy when they left Malden. She had left friends and a Methodist church where she had been active for a strange High Episcopal church and a school in Worcester where teachers did not accept her work although it was correct, claiming she had to use their methods for recording the correct answers.

"Evvie grew into a bright, fair-skinned beauty, adored by Pa and Elsie and me too. She weighed nearly twelve pounds at birth, walked and talked early and, before she was two, she could shinny up lampposts."

According to Ma, baby Evelyn was increasingly admired by the extended family, friends, and neighbors. Laura—my Grandma and Evelyn, Elsie and Dorothy's mother—feared this child would be spoiled. Her father and other relatives were indulging her. It seems Gram tried to counter their lavish attention, so she treated the little girl harshly and little Evvie began to act meanly.

"She'd say I hit her. I'd never do that! If Elsie and I went off to have a good time with our friends, Evvie would pout and fuss and Pa would make us take her along. When we met with our group, she'd have a tantrum and we'd have to leave before the outing was over. I think she was jealous because we had big girl privileges. She was twelve years younger, for heaven's sake! We were punished when she fibbed and said I'd struck her or we'd left her unattended while we went off with boys."

The big sisters felt bitter because the little one they were once so proud of, became a teller of tales and deliberately got them into trouble. Dorothy lost all favor with her father and became angered by her mother's lack of trust. Her baby sister, once fascinating, remained the 'favorite' in everyone's eyes but Gram's. As the big sisters, Elsie and Dorothy, became socially active in their teen years, they longed for more freedom. When their little sister lied, they were forbidden to attend events with their friends.

These losses never stopped. Ma hated school and left in the eight grade. Her dream of being an interior decorator evaporated with the reality of *Negroes* need not apply. Dorothy decided to leave her father's house as soon as she possibly could.

I could understand how Dorothy had arrived at this place—this place where she could shake her finger at a benign monkey, then wring her hands and utter bitter words of hate. Young Dorothy had held onto old resentments and took her mother's admonitions seriously when she left her girlhood home to marry.

"Dorothy! Now you will bear and forbear." That was the only good-bye she got from her mother. My mother became a woman who had lost all expectation of being cared for or about. The role she chose was that of victim. Her mother's caveat about marriage, and Ma's reasons for leaving home to marry were often ominously

repeated to me.

***

Courtship was her ticket to a new life and her suitor was "Beel" Perkins, but marriage brought her a heap of unimaginable misery and disappointment. All this happened long before she met my father, but she placed all her past wrongs and disappointments onto the present situation.

Over the years, her trail of losses grew. She not only lost the favor of her father; her first husband left under miserable circumstances and her baby son had died. Her other child with Mr. Perkin—a daughter—she had ruefully given to the Perkins family to rear. She'd felt bound to give that daughter a chance to be cherished. (Ma did blame some of her troubles on Herbert, the second man she'd married in hopes of improving her life. According to Ma, Herbert negated his promise to parent her first little girl as his own, once *his* first child was born) but she lamented that all of life had become sheer misery and then began to blame her poor lot in life on her second daughter, Audrey. Dorothy claimed she would have become a hairdresser or had some other occupation if it weren't for this troublesome third child.

Now Shirley, this grown, defiant daughter—the one who looked like the Barrow clan; this golden child, this good person wanted to leave her loving home to find out who and what her father was. This one, me—was going to walk out of her house. Both my mother and sister Audrey had fears about my decision to go to Germany. Ma had pleaded, "How can you do this to me after all I've done? How can you betray me like this?"

111

I tried to explain, "I want to know him. I want to understand for myself who he really is and what he's all about. I'm going to accept his offer and go to Germany." Ma could not grasp why her child would want to leave her home to discover anything about the father who had abandoned his family to leave them in abject poverty. My decision defeated my mother, ending in a situation that confounded the entire family.

"You see," my father the Colonel had said, "you're still a minor, not yet twenty-one and because of military rules, you can come to Germany as a dependent of the U. S. Army and get to see some of Europe."

There was a hint of regret or perhaps, guilt in the offer: an opportunity for the Colonel to make amends to the children of his youth whom he had dubbed his "spring" children. He had been "Captain Barrow" when he lived with us in Worcester years before. He'd already had one wife before Dorothy, but no children. Hazel—wife number three—had been quite helpful to Herbert's abandoned young family, but she too was history and I was ready to meet wife number four. The opportunity to travel courtesy of the Army made good sense to me as a young adult however, sister Audrey was fearful. This man had never kept his promises. He had always put himself first and never heeded the consequences to others. I would write him and sometimes he'd not only answer but would send money if that is what I'd asked for. He had brutalized his firstborn when his second was born. One minute he was proudly walking Audrey to school after the late bell and the next minute slapping her to the floor for standing on a box, just because I wanted to stand on the box. He favored me unabashedly and struck out at my mother and sister. This man was

112

completely *unpredictable in the kind of attention he gave Audrey, his first born child. He had succeeded in life yet failed miserably in domestic relationships. He never stopped trying to succeed—he married five times!*

Audrey did not trust this man. She had become my protector and could not tolerate the thought of her sister going alone to this man's home. Dorothy's railings didn't force her decision to go to Germany with me; Audrey had felt it was extremely important to protect her little sister—her naïve, trusting, goody-two-shoes, eleven-month-younger sister. Ginny and Madelyn, our City Hospital classmates, had agreed with me or else Dorothy might have had apoplexy and died when her two girls got on that ship and sailed off to Germany.

"This is a tremendous opportunity Mrs. Barrow! We'll look after you and we'll be your daughters while they're away."

They brought her fish and chips on Friday and picked up all the routines and rituals this depressed woman had clung to and expected of her own daughters. She had relied on us, her daughters to define her reason for living.

***

In September of 1952 Germany was a mind-boggling experience for Audrey and me. We met wife number four, our sisters and a new brother who spoke no English. We went to Paris on the International Train and to Rome. We shopped, bought lederhosen and a modest number of souvenirs. People of color were a novelty in Germany; not so in Paris or Rome. Once, while looking into a store window in Stuttgart, we saw the reflections of a crowd of faces standing behind us, gawking. It was frightening. We went to Stuttgart often enough, but we lived in Viengen, a lush, rural suburb. Our father's assigned housing was typical field grade officer's quarters—a grand house, suitable for wealthy Germans or the officers and gentlemen assigned to the postwar 7th Army Headquarters. Large marble windowsills made comfortable places where we could sit and gaze upon fields and farmlands. Honey wagons fertilized the fields. Looking out the side windows I could see a neighboring house where two girls lived, Sigrid and Uta. They came over to play and taught us German games to the tune of ring-around-a rosy.

"Ring-aring-ariah, da foos iz en der brier."

A cook prepared the meals and did light housekeeping and the chimney sweep came on a regular schedule. By November, I was speaking German by mimicking the sounds without always understanding what I was saying. Audrey could understand more than I could, but she was shy about using the language. German nursemaids cared for the children. Baby Herbert spoke only German and Anita, the youngest little girl of my father's "autumn" children, was bilingual. The other sister, Linda, was the child of my father's fourth wife. She attended a GI School for Dependents' children. They spoke English there but everyone except the Colonel spoke some German at the house in Viengen.

I had an expensive Zeiss Ikon German camera and the Colonel had a darkroom where we could develop our own photographs. We were surrounded by plenty and we took day trips, ate in gourmet restaurants and lacked for nothing. We saw Paris, the Palais De

Versailles, and went to the *Folies Bergere*. We wandered all over Rome from piazza to piazza, gazed at the ceiling in the Sistine Chapel by day and at midnight strolled into Barberini Square, a place which women of the night were known to frequent. Audrey and I were not approached to render services but were smiled at as innocents and were given a bouquet of violets. At Christmas, cousin Danny—who was stationed in Munich—came to spend the holidays. More feasts, more gifts, more stark contrasts to life on Ellen Street. I gained about ten pounds and the weight of abundance reached a climax.

Something was very wrong. All this? *All this and more?* It was a deep question, pushing its way up from my toes. My mind began to fixate on the disparity between my life in Germany and my life at home.

January came, bringing with it a severe strain of influenza. Audrey had a beau now. We sisters had been chauffeured in the Colonel's car as we didn't drive, so our father would enlist a select few of his men on base to escort his daughters. The car with its flags fluttering would approach the gatehouse at Army Headquarters and every man would salute upon recognizing the Colonel's vehicle. Quite a few of the soldiers had taken a liking to us girls. I, naïve and inexperienced with men, thought of the young soldiers as big brothers. The men, amazed by my innocence, brought me a book about sex that had information about my dormant organs and then they invited me to experience sexual sensations.

"You mean you never had an orgasm? You don't know what an orgasm is?"

I knew about anatomy and physiology, but nursing

115

school hadn't dealt with human sexuality. Exploring wasn't that appealing, but I did read the book. Being saluted at the Post was more exciting to me than sex; living in the lap of luxury satiated my whole being. Life was good.

By February, the soldiers wanted to date seriously and one of the men had begun to court my sister. He wanted this extraordinary girl for his wife. The thought was unsettling to me. Audrey married? The GI lived in New Jersey and the idea of not having my sister at my side was unimaginable. The family was talking about going home. Little Linda had the flu and was so ill and dehydrated that they had to admit her to the 7th Army Hospital. Everyone was sick with the flu. My father had taken to his bed, Linda was back home and I was nursing myself back to health. It was a time for us all to slow down, a time to reflect and look ahead to the future. We were going back to the States.

Wrong! Wrong! Wrong! Something was *terribly* wrong. My mind began to race. I thought about the house on Ellen Street: about digging a new pit for the outhouse, carrying water from the neighbor's silcock and lugging kerosene to keep the black stove working and to fill the lamps.

Wrong! Wrong! Wrong! Unjust! Unfair! I could not contain the fury that was rising within me. It must have been something my father said. He would often brag about his "spring" children and even made complimentary remarks about my mother, Dorothy: what a good job she had done bringing us up.

"Let me see your teeth." He offered to have any needed dental work done on the base. *How could he ignore everything else? Didn't he know the depth of our poverty? Couldn't he understand what a young woman of twenty-one might feel about having no running water or electricity? It was 1953, for God's sake!*

I stormed into his bedroom and proceeded to tell him how very angry it made me to think about his neglect. His lack of response increased my fury. I decided I should kill him but the impact of that decision paralyzed my legs. I could not move. I was at his bedside and reached for his throat, glaring into his dumbfounded eyes. His face looked desperate and he lost control of his bowels. My rage turned to fear and confusion. Emma was alongside him, wide eyed and silent. My raised voice must have alerted Audrey and Danny that something strange was happening. I don't recall any real panic from anyone—just tears and gentle assistance. With Audrey's and Danny's help, I got to the hospital. I don't recall if my stepmother or my father accompanied us. One large, blue-green capsule slipped me into oblivion. The next day I was wheeled to the neurology ward and met with a physician who explained what had happened the night before.

"You had hysterical paralysis—tell me about your sex life."

"My what?" What was he talking about? I left his office and found my way back to the neurology unit. The paralysis was totally gone. I complained about the doctor's disrespectful approach and was assigned a new physician. Those therapy sessions went well. I wrote to my mother telling her of my illness and good progress.

When my father and sister came to visit, shortly after my recovery process began, they informed my doctor that they wanted me discharged. The Colonel explained, "We have to ship out next week."

"She should stay here and continue her therapy. She's making such good progress."

I had my say; "I'll stay—it's OK. I have a good therapist now. I had so much anger and confusion about so many things, but I'm sorting it all out. I'll be fine."

"No! No! We all have to go at the same time as the Army will get us all back together. I don't know how I can get you home after the ship leaves."

The Colonel and his oldest daughter argued, they pleaded, they threatened. They won. The household was packed, crated and stored aboard ship. Everything I bought came back whole except one dainty finger on a figurine that I mended easily. The most prized of my souvenirs was a bright green, glazed ceramic monkey, about twelve inches tall that was designed to hold liquor.

But I was not yet whole. I had written to my mother and told her about the gentle therapist they finally found for me; about the crafts I'd made; about my plan to get outpatient psychiatric care when I got home. I was still figuring out how to cope with my righteous indignation that had erupted into a paralyzing urge to kill.

Aboard ship the sea churned and tossed and seasickness made the long journey torture. From Germany, the boat went to Newfoundland to drop off some airmen. The baby's crib ricocheted about the cabin and we had to tie it to the bunks. I couldn't sleep. The railed mess table couldn't contain the dishes; they poured water on the tablecloth to keep the plates and silverware from lurching up and down the dining table. I couldn't hold anything down except Jell-O. I stayed on deck sunup to sundown. It made for less cleanup and the air seemed to help, no matter the cold. I lost more than a pound a day and the weight of abundance was gone forever. There was only loss, deprivation and struggle to look forward to.

We finally docked in New York and I went to sleep. The Colonel was officer of the day and thus was required to remain on board ship until everyone disembarked. Sleep was my new luxury.

"Wake up! Wake up!" My sister's voice was frantic. She shook and shouted until I finally opened my eyes. I felt as if I was dreaming. "Ma's here! She's waiting on the dock!"

I heard the words but only felt rage well up throughout my body. Let me sleep! For the love of God, I need to sleep! I did not speak it aloud but rose in a trance to look out onto the dock. I waved; I felt glad, yet the turmoil I felt inside never left. Hours went by and Dorothy's feet were freezing. We threw our fur-lined German boots over the side for our mom. Darkness came. There was a billeting problem.

"But Colonel, we only have transportation and quarters for your wife, two daughters and yourself!"

There were two wives, four daughters and a son waiting impatiently for transportation and a place to sleep. It took a heap of sorting out, but the two families got to Fort Dix, New Jersey. My mother and my sister and I finally arrived in Worcester. I stayed awake, kept moving and kept unpacking.

"You didn't get my letters? You didn't know I was in the hospital? I wrote to you!"

They began to plead with me.

"Go to bed. Get some rest."

119

"No! There are things that need to be done around here." I'd unpacked my decanter. The green monkey's melody soothed my disquieted spirit. No matter what they shouted, no matter how much they pleaded, I did not intend to be told what to do ever again.

***

On this day some six months after we had left for Germany, Ma stared at her once dutiful daughter, the one who had passively and lovingly listened to all her tales of misery—this meek one who had picked up a hatchet and announced, "Don't bother me! I'm going to chop down the brush between here and Gram's. It's all overgrown. I *know* what I want to do. *You* can't tell me what to do any more!"

Rage distorted my face as I walked out the door and the room filled with silent panic. Ma and my sister were there. Aunt Evvie might have been there. If my recollection of that weird day is accurate, soon trusted neighbors, the Wellwoods, were there too.

"Call Dr. Hall!"—rang out the first suggestion.

"Call Father McKenzie," rang out another. "Something awful has happened to Shirley!"

CHAPTER 20

M. H. S. Survivor

My early visits to Worcester City Hospital were brief and, except for the tonsillectomy and an embarrassing ride home, I usually came home feeling just fine. I rode home from City Hospital with a social worker when we had our tonsils out. We were admitted together for the surgery and had to stay overnight. Audrey had fine tonsils, but some zealous surgeon decided she might as well be admitted and butchered along with me. I had been plagued with severe colds and chronic tonsillitis. That's how I got familiar with hospitals. The embarrassment happened on a rare occasion when my father came to bring me home from the hospital after one of the many upper respiratory ailments.

It's daddy. I wonder how long he's been home? What a surprise! He's giving the nurse a brown paper bag with my real clothes. It won't be long now, and I'll be home! Uh oh, there's all my things, but where's my underpants? Oh no, he left them home!

I used to get carsick so I lay down on the back seat to keep my stomach calm. Father always drives fast and hard. Surely, Saint Christopher rides on his shoulders, hanging on tight all the way. It was one of his wild driving moments that bounced me off the seat into a bottoms-up pile on the car floor. Pedestrians waiting to cross Chandler Street at the corner of Madison most likely never saw me scrambling to cover my exposure. None the less, it was mortifying.

***

By 1953, Worcester City Hospital was my alma mater. Part of my nurses' training had been a three-month affiliation at Worcester State Hospital, so it seemed logical to go the State Hospital and continue the therapy initiated at the 7th Army Hospital in Germany. I understood that the paralyzing episode I had in Stuttgart was related to the accumulation of stifled little-girl rage and years of deprivation plus my new fear of losing my closeness to the sister with whom I grew up. She was planning to marry one of the soldiers we met in Germany. My Army therapist and I had been able to talk about how coping with stress as well as contracting influenza contributed to the episode. That is why it seemed so confusing when the family—my mother, sister and my father—was so opposed when I announced my plan to admit myself as a voluntary out-patient at Worcester State Hospital.

When they stopped arguing about who to blame for my need to be hospitalized, they sent me to Worcester *City* Hospital. While their "what-should-we-do" plans continued to be made, I grew more confused and more annoyed that my own plans were not being considered.

"What day is it? What's taking so much time? Where am I? This is not what I planned! It looks like the old Woodward Wing. It's a private, comfortable place with homelike furnishings and a window with a plain, uninteresting view. Is that a parking lot? I used to work this

122

wing all by myself, guess I never had time to look out the window. There's somebody sitting in the chair next to my bed. Is it Bernie?"

Bernadine McCann was my favorite nursing instructor. Bernadine's face was bright red and she stared at me for a long while as if she was waiting for me to tell her something. She began to talk. I wondered how long she'd been waiting there.

"Why are you doing this?" My instructor spoke softly.

"Doing what?" I focused on her crimson face while a memory flash—like a movie cut—put me in the picture: *I was slapping Bernadine's face repeatedly!*

"I don't know. I just don't know." My voice seemed to belong to someone else, just as this unexplainable action had come from a place that my brain could no longer command.

Someone else had been in that room, asking strange questions. I was listening to the radio. Questions—even the radio was singing questions: "Who was the doggie in the window? Who put that doggie in the window?" *Was I the doggie in the window?*

I just sat there. It was an intern with a familiar face and a funny name, Lightbody. He stared at me as I sat on the window ledge. He too asked what I was doing and why. *Wasn't I supposed to be there?* In that fleeting moment, I realized my body and mind had taken leave of each other.

With Father McKenzie's help, decisions were quickly made and finances arranged. Private duty nurses were provided around the clock until my transfer to the Brattleboro Retreat in Vermont. Real became surreal, and whimsical thoughts became senseless actions. The

123

long ride to Vermont was an ordeal for everyone.

This is a special ride and I have a secret mission. I'm supposed to exterminate my father. That's what this ride to nowhere is about. I wonder who planned it? Who is going to help carry out the plan? How am I supposed to do it? My boots! I'll kick the back of his head. That will do it!

My boot-shod feet flew at the back of my father's head as he drove the car. My cousin Daniel used words and muscle to contain my irrational attack. There were other family members in the car but my memory splintered, spluttered and blanked like a local radio wave losing its signal the further I went from home.

Bits and pieces of reality tumbled into my senses on arrival: the admission shower that matted my smoothly pressed hair, the big, brawny, women with ruddy grinning faces who twisted my arm in order to march me from upstairs to the chaotic lower room where control was imposed. I wore a canvas jacket that wrapped my arms securely around my waist and tied in back. The jacket limited all upper-body motion as I paced about the room. My body heat intensified. I wriggled and sweated then sat down on my tethered hands, slid them under my buttocks, untied the knots with my teeth, then imitated the position. I did not sleep or eat and I was forced to lie down. The attendants jammed an enamel spouted pot against my gritted teeth. *Was it melted cherry ice cream?* I moved more slowly, the arm-twisting and jacketing stopped and I was taken upstairs.

A genteel woman worked tirelessly on my matted hair and braided it in a crown around my head. The worker wore braids, neatly covered by a crinoline

Mennonite cap. There was a bright dining area where meals were served on flowery china plates. My sleeping room was dark and small.

That dumb waiter in the kitchen, why is it near my bedroom? That dumb waiter is waiting to snatch me somewhere down in the dark . . . to a furnace . . . to burn to charcoal. Who will save me? Who knows about this terrible plan?

Routinely, I sat with the others outside the treatment room door. From the wooden bench-like chairs, we took turns hurrying to the lavatory where the stench of fear-diarrhea lingered long after everyone disappeared into the room. In that room I was strapped to a table-bed, a glob of jell was placed on my temples, then a white, blinding slap hurled me into a lifeless chasm.

I stood on a loading platform, staring at a small cluster of women. I was wearing a strange short-sleeved dress and in my hand I cradled a cigarette.

"What on earth am I doing here?"

One of the attendants came towards me.

"How are you feeling today? You're doing so much better."

I had no notion of who this woman was or what she meant by "so much better."

After viewing half of a movie, I found myself back downstairs sweating in a canvas jacket. Numberless worried nights and listless days slid together. There were scraps of memory: sitting on a young male attendant's lap; more waiting outside the treatment room door with silent, blank-faced people. I drifted into the foul lavatory from the chairs and was led dumbly to the litter-bed, then jarred senseless by a blind snap of white light. It happened many times.

My mother gave me a prayer written on a letter-sized pink paper with tiny scalloped edges. I repeated it again and again as I paced the corridor.

"I will lift up mine eyes unto the hills, from whence cometh my strength. My foes press on from every side. Thine aid supply, thy strength bestow. Oh saving victim opening wide the gates . . . " I read, silently recited and paced for days at a time. On one of Father McKenzie's visits, he paced with me.

I talked with my therapist and began to remember from one day to the next until they began to piece together. I went home for a weekend and all went well. With my sister and classmates, I went out to eat and listened to music on the jukebox. At the Retreat, the doctors began discharge-planning. The church helped with finances and my sister and mother began to relax.

Unexpectedly, I was summoned to the superintendent's office. Dr. Zawocky informed me that I was being discharged into the care of my mother. This was not the plan. When I saw my stepmother sitting in the office, confusion swelled to indignation.

"She's not my *mother*! She is ***not*** my mother!"

"My, my. Now don't get so upset," the superintendent advised.

My stepmother insisted that she was in fact the mother and the family had made this decision. I was to go with her to my father's home on Cape Cod. I argued furiously to no avail. Dr. Zawocky reached a point where he simply wanted us both to go: to go anywhere out of his office. My belongings were brought and we were escorted out of the Retreat. In a full state of fury, I threatened my stepmother's life and insisted on being driven home to Worcester. Then the hellish nightmare came full circle—my sister and mother demanded to know why I had been discharged early. The explanation: money. My father had been sent a bill. It was apparently shocking and a hasty decision had been made. My father was summoned and, when he came to Worcester, accusations and blame flew in all directions. It was a rerun of the earlier chaos upon the homecoming from Germany. Unable to contain my rage, I terrified them again.

"What are we to do now?" They were sure they could not contain me. Hospitalization was the only answer. I was driven halfway down to Cape Cod to the Taunton State Hospital. I found myself on a back ward.

How long have I been here? Has it been a week? I don't need a damned shower! This is humiliating! Oh yes, the admission shower. I'm in this systematic ritual where one is stripped of every possession and of all dignity.

The next thirty days went quickly. My dignity was gone, but I held onto my voice. "I do not want this Dilantin and Phenobarbital. I will not take it!"

The correct identification of the pills and my conviction caught the attention of the affiliate student nurses.

"This is your seizure medication—you do have seizures, don't you?"

Where did they get that notion? Was I raving, ranting and throwing tantrums in the admission room? Had I been rolling on a cold tile floor?

There was no shock therapy and I would not take medications. One clear recollection I had was of being bound hand and foot in bed. I lay quietly for a long time, then decided I did not need this kind of control.

My complete awareness returned. I felt under the mattress edge, inspected the knots, leaned and wriggled my hand free. Easily freeing my legs, I noticed several other women who were restrained in their beds. They were all lying quietly. Unnoticed and undisturbed by the preoccupied staff, I got out of my bed, sat and talked with my fellow inmates. Several assured me that they felt in full control so I untied all but one: Patricia, who felt angry and unsure. We talked. From that meeting we became friends and kept in touch for years after we both left the hospital. I was never put in restraints again.

No longer enraged, I quickly earned privileges, assumed responsibility and gained recognition. The nurses made it known to the treatment team that this articulate brown girl was a professional nurse. At their suggestion and with their support, I was given opportunities to help with the nursing care of bedridden patients. This approach and their respect led to rapid return to "self" and to recovery. Patricia and I knit ankle socks. I learned how to do a cable stitch and to use four double-pointed needles. Within thirty days I went home to Worcester.

Women—especially women of color trying to cope with rage—do not fare well in the system. The mental health system no longer spewed its harshness on me. My role as a health consumer was quickly reversed from being a consumer to being a provider. That same summer of 1953 a plan was in place for me to take a nursing position at an Episcopal summer camp in Charlton. Father McKenzie and the administration felt confident that I could ease back into full-time work at summer's end. I could study for my board exams and enjoy the woodsy environment. Nature had another plan. My ability to survive and the completeness of my recovery were amazingly put to the test before I could accept the camp job.

A violent storm spewing hail, crashing thunder and swirling havoc tore across Worcester County. It was June 9, 1953. My mother and I were standing on Pleasant Street, waiting for the evening bus home. The bright, setting sun was shadowed by a massive, smoky-black cloud that gave the sky an unearthly look. The still air felt thick. The summer's heat paused as rain and hail crashed to the streets in furious, blinding sheets. At home, safe and dried off, we heard the bad news on the radio.

"A deadly tornado has just passed through the Great Brook Valley Housing Projects. It has followed a mile-wide path through the County, touched down again at Assumption Preparatory School. There are reports of fatalities at Assumption!" The commentator's frightened voice pleaded for nurses and doctors to report to duty. "The National Guard will escort rescue workers through the traffic-jam of delivery trucks and other makeshift ambulances."

Hospitals were flooded with victims. Winslow Surgery was designated a temporary morgue. I reported for duty. Medical personnel worked throughout the night, taking no breaks, relieved only by professional volunteers like myself. In eighty-four minutes, ninety-four lives had been lost and fifteen thousand people had become homeless. Hired on the spot, Winslow Surgery became my permanent assignment and I began full-time work. It was a wonderful place to work. The team spirit and effort of that terrible day was a hallmark of the care given in that old amphitheater that was once the only surgery room. It was the minor surgery now where plaster casts were put on, burns were dressed, toenails and tonsils were removed, and other procedures requiring brief anesthesia were performed. A dark cloud brought me there, but color never seemed to matter in Winslow surgery. I loved working there.

CHAPTER 21

Angst Robed in Black and White

My AARP magazine invited readers to share stories about work. One suggestion made was to describe your most difficult boss. Inspired, I wrote about Sister Eleanor Jean and mailed it off. I never heard from the magazine, yet it enabled me to revisit a flood of memories.

It was 1956 and I was searching for a job which would advance my professional career. The nursing profession was changing. Three-year hospital-based diploma programs had dominated the nursing field, but the future clearly pointed in the direction of college-based degree programs for the professional nurse; the rationale being, *all* professionals will have college degrees. At Worcester City Hospital, nurses with bachelor's and master's degrees were paid more than those with diplomas and were placed in positions of leadership. Although they lacked clinical experience, they persevered and soon earned my respect. My search for a nursing job that also offered an opportunity to earn a bachelor of nursing degree brought me to Washington, DC. My interview with the Director of Nurses at Georgetown University Hospital was as gracious and pleasant as springtime.

I had spent several springs in Washington, DC. The

cherry blossoms were in bloom and it was a beautiful time to visit the Nation's Capital. My father and his fourth wife lived in Washington. Our relationship had improved with time and I lodged with him and his family when I went for my interview at Georgetown University Hospital. This hospital, right in the middle of metropolitan Washington, DC, had an agreement with the Catholic University called the *Learn and Earn* plan, which allowed staff nurses to work while studying for their degree in nursing. Paid on-duty time and class study time were carefully coordinated. I researched many degree programs and this one was unique: a perfect fit for my career plans. It was a refreshing distance from Worcester and my father had introduced Audrey and me to some interesting fellows when we visited Washington one Cherry Blossom time. They were attending Howard University with him and were brothers close to our age. The Carter brothers called each other by nicknames. Oscar, the oldest was called O.D., which was short for Oscar Dillihan and his brother "Thiddo" was called Tayed. It took a while before I realized that was the way folks in Alabama said Theodore and Ted. After one date, Audrey dumped O.D., dated Ted once and had no further interest in either of them but I liked them both.

I successfully applied for and was awarded a Federal Grant designed to attract minorities into the health fields and it would pay my full tuition at University. My interview with the director of nurses at Georgetown University Hospital was a complete contrast from my first nursing interview with Margaret Dieter at Worcester City Hospital in 1949.

The Nursing Director at Georgetown University Hospital cordially invited me to share my nursing goals and assisted me to quickly gain reciprocity at the DC Nursing Registry. My Massachusetts Registration would be valid in the District of Columbia after I retook the obstetrical test and met the required top score. I was hired and we agreed that my assignment would be on the maternity unit and I could review and retake the exam without difficulty. She gave me the name of their nurse-liaison at Catholic University and the interview was over. I thanked her and rose to leave. Before I reached the door, she called to me,

"By the way Miss Barrow, on your application, you put a capital C for race." She paused. "What does that stand for?" We were both smiling when I exited with my well-rehearsed answer, "colored, of course!"

Among the many interesting people I met at Georgetown, the most perplexing person was the nursing supervisor. She never smiled. Sister Eleanor Jean swooshed onto the ward every morning, her many-layered habit struggling to keep pace with her ageless, agile body. In 1957, the Georgetown University Hospital was managed by an order of nursing nuns. They guarded supplies, oversaw time sheets and supervised all aspects of the Nursing Service. Sister Eleanor Jean was my boss in the maternity unit. My work-mates didn't seem to have issues with this nun. Her prudent—verging on miserly—distribution of supplies was in keeping with the other nursing nuns. The cleanliness and efficiency of the maternity ward was clear evidence of their care and concern and a hallmark of this nursing order.

As the newest nurse on the ward, my orientation clarified the authority and responsibilities of the nuns and also my role as a staff nurse. It was a great assignment. The maternity ward was usually a joyous place to work, even if patients were sometimes anxious or in medically alarming states, but generally the miracle of birth created an emotionally positive atmosphere. But my boss, Sister Eleanor Jean, appeared incapable of experiencing any cheer. She was particularly indifferent in my presence: less serene, and noticeably cryptic. She would count cereal boxes she had carefully locked in a little pantry where the patient's snack foods were kept. The chain she put on the cupboard doors at the end of the day proved to be only a wee challenge to my ability to wiggle the cereal boxes out with the aid of a ruler and fingers. It was like guiding pennies out of a piggy-bank.

"Did you use supplies from the pantry last night?" Her tone was always accusatory.

"Oh yes, we had several admissions tonight, and Mrs. Blank was ravenous after her delivery." I would always own up cheerfully to using the supplies and had quickly learned how to access whatever my patients needed. My honesty seemed to infuriate her. It was not unusual for us to run out of sanitary supplies for new admissions. Those supplies were secured in another inaccessible closet. I'd have go to the delivery room and ask for necessary items: sanitary napkins, blankets—whatever.

There was also an early morning ritual of serving Holy Communion to any Catholic mother desiring this sacrament. The nursing protocol covering this pre-dawn ritual was to identify those mothers by turning on the lamp over their beds. The priest could then go efficiently to each patient in the darkness without awakening her roommate. Sister Eleanor Jean would follow the priest to assist him with the administration of the sacrament. She was often late. The priest would wait for her, and while the sacred elements and the priest were present in the hallway, no person was permitted to enter the hall. If I had to meet a patient's needs and entered the hallway, I was instructed to bow to my knees and remain there until Sister arrived. At least once a week this process interrupted my ability to give morning care and also delayed the nursery's schedule for bringing newborns to their mothers for feeding.

After one extended delay, I asked Sister Eleanor Jean how we might remedy this disruption in patient care. Her fixed, wide-eyed stare informed me that no other nurse had considered the serving of Mass a nursing disruption, or if they *had* entertained this thought, they never dared to ask a nun to consider a creative solution. After a ghastly pause she blinked and, in a piercing, sharp tone, fired her curt response.

"When Father is late, we all must wait! If you want a remedy, you go talk with him!" She sailed off down the highly polished floors as if she were propelled from behind. It did not occur to me at the time that her answer was a threat or even a rhetorical response used to dismiss the issue. I was sincere in seeking a solution and took her suggestion literally, so I immediately went to the priest who came up with a splendid solution: he gave me instructions on how to assist him. It was a perfect remedy. He was predictably on time; I had my patients identified, the communion box in place and was at the elevator waiting. The following day, Sister came much later than usual. Morning care was complete and the hungry infants were being carried to their waiting mothers.

135

She shrieked at me, "Where's Father?"

"He was early today and left at five thirty." My voice betrayed my surprise at her venomous tone.

"He couldn't have!" she protested. She gasped, and then bustled off the ward as if the end of the world was beginning on the spot where I stood. From then on, my fate was sealed; she despised me. Not a day went by that Sister Eleanor Jean did not interrogate me. Her vengeance never stopped. If it wasn't the counting of supplies, it was the spot of dirt on my shoe or the reason why a patient was admitted to this room and not that one. If she missed morning report, she would call me at home, waking me from my sleep to ask a trivial question. I was a new nurse introducing a new era, and my boss had heard the knell of doom. She saw in me a preview of a scenario she had never before imagined: a black professional nurse at Georgetown University Hospital.

Despite this harassment, my experience remained positive. My work-mates and the doctors were patient-oriented, highly professional and personally supportive. *They* were keenly aware of the change I represented but that I could barely perceive. It was not simply my crinoline nurse's cap and Boston accent that caused the staff to dub me the "Yankee" nurse. It was a change beyond my comprehension.

Desegregation had come to Washington, DC. The bathroom doors had just been refinished in order to remove the *white* and *colored* designations. They had never before hired a colored nurse in the history of this prestigious hospital. That was my status: the first black registered nurse, and there was nothing I could have said or done to dispel Sister Eleanor Jean's hatred.

***

When a new mother was admitted on my shift for observation, I placed her in the empty bed nearest the nurse's station. A soft, unmonitored uterus could cause a woman to silently bleed to death. Nursing assistants—who were all black females—appeared confused. One night when I grumbled in frustration being unable to locate new patients predictably the night after I admitted them, an aide looked at me suspiciously.

"You mean, you really don' know?"

I continued to complain. "Look, they moved three or four people and there were no new admissions today. That's a lot of work and it makes no sense!"

The aide called her buddy from the adjoining unit.

"Clara, you won' believe this, but uh Yankee nurse don' know why we been movin' all theeze patients roun'!"

They explained the mystery. The hospital never placed black patients in semiprivate rooms with white patients. When my first baby was born at Georgetown University Hospital, my roommate was white. The nursing staff had given up trying to juggle beds. My last rude awakening came when I asked for my daughter's Georgetown birth certificate. One of the night nurse's responsibilities was to fill in the demographic data of the new deliveries onto beautiful, parchment, scrolled birth certificates, that were then tied with a narrow ribbon. The nuns would complete them and give them to the mothers the day they went home. I did not know that the black mothers had never received the ones I had prepared for them. I was informed on the day that

I was discharged, that those parchment certificates were never given to black mothers. I was given a municipal agency address to request my baby's birth certificate.

Innocence, honesty and professionalism had made my experience there a good one. Thank heavens I never again had such a difficult boss as Sister Eleanor Jean.

The Other Mrs. Barrow with her Children & Shirley

O. D. and Shirley with Dog, Worcester

CHAPTER 22

Longing, Loving and Living on My Own

I longed for my father and finally did the work necessary to build a relationship with him. Healing that old hurt allowed me to open my heart to men. My mother's sad history and my father's pattern of seeking beautiful, intelligent women, then abandoning one to make way for the next, led me to believe my parents' way of life was not the life for me. Marriage was not an option—I would be a career woman. I earned my diploma in nursing and then found that teaching hospital near Washington DC where my father lived. He put me up temporarily then helped me find a place of my own in Georgetown. I began working on the third shift. It was convenient when I first arrived because I used my father's car for transportation. Before the household got in gear for the day, I was off duty and at home getting ready for bed.

Oscar, the young man my father had introduced me to, became seriously amorous. We began dating while I was still at 1313 Farragut Street, NW: my father's house. I had walked many blocks to my father's house when O.D.'s passion had exceeded mine. O.D. lived with his brother Ted at 1023 Fairmont Street, NW—alphabet blocks away. One evening when his brother was not at home, Oscar became aggressively passionate. I was outraged at his plan to make me "catch up" with him. He left the room momentarily, laughing at my dismay. I left the apartment, walked off the main avenue and got myself safely to Farragut Street. I was steaming mad and didn't want Oscar to drive up the avenue and try any more nonsense! Hours later, my stepmother let him into the house and implored me to speak with him. He was upset and in a state of disbelief at my actions. I was angry with her for letting him in the house!

My father found me an apartment on 2727 P Street within walking distance to Georgetown University Hospital—no need for a car. The suburb was beautiful, with little boutiques, shops and an Episcopal Church just down the brick sidewalk. When I walked home from work there were few people out and about. I greeted milkmen and engineers up on poles or workers in manholes repairing wires and pipes. Some mornings I attended Matins, the early church service, or slipped in at Vespers after sleeping the day away. On frosty mornings the bricks made walking a slippery adventure. Past freezes and frost heaves made humps in quaint walkways and required the pedestrian to remain alert. This change in season brought caution in other areas of my life. Georgetown University Hospital had that special learn-and-earn plan: learn at Catholic University; earn good wages at Georgetown University Hospital. It was a unique design, created to help RNs earn a baccalaureate as well as advanced degrees in nursing. The admissions clerk at the Catholic University refused my application. Catholic University did not accept colored students. *How dare they call themselves a Catholic University! Spouting Christianity and practicing segregation!* My approved Federal Grant covering full tuition was of no interest to them. I was referred to the University of Maryland. I felt lied to and betrayed again. My sweet life felt spoiled and sour for days—my glorious independence had run into a few humps.

Now I was in my own place, O.D.'s adoration and attention soothed my wounded spirit and dulled my disappointment. I had never experienced such attention before and willingly surrendered to his loving tutelage. It was a great adventure and an exploration into sexuality, but with no intercourse—my religious programming forbade the ultimate act. We planned to marry; accordingly, a new avenue appeared on my map of life. O.D. and I were making plans for a June wedding, and I suggested to my sister that we make it a double wedding. Choosing wedding gowns and selecting dates was very exciting. O.D. and I agreed to support each other in our educational pursuits. His ultimate goal was a Doctorate in Psychology and mine was a Bachelor of Science in Nursing. I had already been derailed by Catholic University. The Earn and Learn agreement between Georgetown and Catholic University was no longer feasible since it required that I commute to Maryland, and that voided the Hospital's promise to schedule my working hours to allow compatible study hours. A miraculous surprise froze my path and shocked me into yet another avenue.

"Well, Miss Barrow, that digestive problem has a simple explanation. You're pregnant." My trusted physician was beaming at me.

"What? What are you saying? Pregnant, that's impossible!" My nursing education did not prepare me for this unimaginable news. Since no angels had whispered to me, I demanded a medical explanation.

"Penetration is not necessary for conception. Let me show you something." He reached for a urine specimen that was sitting in a laboratory tray, awaiting pickup. He drew some urine into an asepto syringe, placed a few drops onto a glass slide, and had me look into a microscope that sat next to a centrifuge. I knew how to use a centrifuge to measure specific gravity of urine.

"What am I looking at? Those tiny pollywog things?" My senses were blunted by disbelief. Black dots with pollywog tails zigzagged in the tiny puddle of urine.

"This is not *my* urine!" He chuckled at the sight of my gaping mouth and tearful eyes.

"Well, certainly you must have been intimate." His tone was gentle as he saw the tears. "Your body fluids in intimacy give these sperm all the moisture they need to swim home. Surely your partner experiences ejaculation? You are looking at sperm. They live for days after ejaculation and they are great swimmers. Look!"

I could no longer see. I could no longer hear much either. When I left the office, fog filled my mind and hovered there. This was a strange path. It was spring again. The trees were budded; blossoms waved in courtyards yet all the beauty was interrupted by sudden waves of nausea and bursts of vomiting. I was a confused, worried wretch. O.D. was excited, amazed and to my surprise, pleased.

"Now we can *really* have sex!" That was not on my agenda. My mind was tortured with unanswered questions: *what about our wedding plans? What must I say to my sister, my priest and my family?* Surely fate had a plan for me that I had not figured out.

"Don't tell them anything!" was O.D.'s solution. "We can go on as planned. You won't even show by June. We can live together now! I won't have to come out to Georgetown. I'll talk to Ted!"

Move in together? Intercourse? No! Tears and fog along with spring rain promised sunshine. Summer would surely come. I was very clear about one thing: before we did anything else, we had to be married. O.D. was not deterred. If those were my conditions, he would meet them. He had already become an Episcopalian, and had met every other expectation or suggestion that I made.

"Let's elope!" He declared, "We can go to Rockville and be married in three days."

That is just what we did, with plan B still in place— we would still go to Massachusetts in June and be married at St. Matthew's. I kept working, worrying and vomiting. This plan was not right. I went to confession. The empathic priest supported my best thinking. It made sense. We announced our condition to everyone who cared about us, canceled our June wedding plans, had our marriage blessed and began to live as man and wife. It was a great relief! In the next three years, 1957, 1958 and 1959 we lived in three states, I experienced three pregnancies, and I learned a great deal about longing, loving, and living.

**Audrey's Wedding Party
with Shirley as Matron of Honor**

CHAPTER 23

Being a Mom

I am so thankful to be my kid's mom.
For my mom, I was a bundle of woes,
times were hard; we barely had food or clothes.
Parenthood is not the act of birth—
it's all the years and all the tears mixed with mirth.
My plan for life included "wife"
but motherhood could wait!
Before we went to college, pregnancy was my fate.
Our best-laid plans were altered by surprise.
Being a mom: once, twice then thrice—my demise?
Never! Our daughters are simple gifts
from the Powers that be—
precious gifts to me,
and my first glimpse of eternity.

Shirley with Baby Daughters

CHAPTER 24

Those Days Are Gone

Spring-cleaning, ironing sheets, making fruit cakes—those days are gone. I used to clean closets every spring and fall, say grace before meals, read bedtime stories and have weekly house-cleaning routines. That was then. The new millennium has come and gone and I look back to the life I used to live; the life when I kept house and brought in frozen clothes and sheets with evening bugs that had been mashed in the jaws of the laundry mangle my old nursing buddy, Sully, had given me. Hard work, night shifts, routines and prayer kept the wolf from my door.

I still keep house in a modified fashion. Cleaning and cooking are no longer the priority they were when I was in charge of all chores as I shared my home with my husband Oscar and our first child, Laura.

Living in the District of Columbia had made me sensitive to heat, humidity, and smells. My visits to DC in the springtime had not prepared me for the pestilence of Washington in the summer. A week of heat and one hundred percent humidity with no relief at night left me collapsed in my bed. Neighbors went out of their houses, onto porches or formed groups that strolled around the block singing spirituals. Others would join in with the *a cappella* strollers to create a celestial chorus.

Death while hearing those voices seemed as if it would be a welcome escape from the heat. Summer was the time when cows grazed on wild scallions and the milk smelled and tasted like onions. Just raising the glass to my nose rapidly triggered my gag reflex. I could not drink it. Morning sickness remained long after the usual three months. After our elopement I moved to O.D.'s place that he shared with his brother. We lived with Ted until the baby was born, then O.D. received a job offer from a state school in Pownal, Maine.

The crisp Maine air kept the three of us, O.D., baby Laurie and me, huddled together in our close quarters in Pownal where we spent our first days alone together. Once we moved to our apartment in Portland, I set up housekeeping. We visited Worcester, showed off our baby Laurie and got a dog from the pound. We named him "Worcester" and maybe that's where he went the first day we let him out the back door. We didn't replace him. Taking care of our baby joyfully took up our time and attention. Spring comes late in Maine but I found the March snow exhilarating in comparison to Washington summers. During those housekeeping years that we lived in Maine, I loved to bake. We added to our scant furnishings and established our first home together. Our apartment at 9 Forest Park overlooked the bay. I thought it was Casco Bay, but it could have been Back Cove. In the early mornings I would look out onto the tidal flats and watch old women with long skirts and aprons, sweeping their hands majestically as they tiptoed along the sand harvesting shellfish. The bilge-like aroma of the flats never offended my olfactory glands as the sea breezes more than compensated for the occasional smell.

We lived in Maine during the winter of 1957 to late summer of 1959. Most of the household chores were mine to do, but O.D. was the meat cook, and he made 'rave-review' chili. We shared childcare yet, if a sitter was needed, it was my job to find one. He was horrid at doing laundry. When he washed navy-blue sweatshirts with white baby diapers, I suspected it was his way of making certain he was never asked to do the laundry again. It took multiple washings, repeated bleaching and much sunshine before the baby's diapers looked decent.

"What have I done now?" The smell of fresh bread put my husband on alert. Kneading bread-dough released tensions that I was not aware of, but O.D. knew I was upset about something. It was usually a misunderstanding or a violation of an agreement about money that caused me to spontaneously bake bread or to grind my teeth at night. The complexities of life had quickly come upon us and money was a constant area of conflict. O.D. had no qualms about writing checks. It mattered not to him if there was money in the account. He used my department store charge account with the same abandon. I took a part-time job at Maine Medical Center in Portland to improve our financial situation and we also became involved with the church. Our baby sitter was a member of our parish. O.D. and I could have verbal agreements about the use of money, but once our situation improved, he would spend without any consultation or a mutual plan. When he bought an expensive boat, I sought counseling from our priest as I had other concerns about his reactions to living in Maine. O.D. had noticed our neighbor and claimed he was the same man who gave the nightly news. I trusted Oscar's thinking yet his behavior was confusing me. He also had a strange reaction to a little neighbor boy, so I was worried.

The boy stood on our back stoop, staring at O.D.

"You're black!" the child declared. O.D. came back into the apartment and shut the door. The little boy stayed outside near our back door and O.D. would not go out. He didn't go to work that day. I worried about him. As it turned out, our adult neighbor *was* the local newscaster, but other worrisome behavior arose. One evening as he lay on the couch, he blurted out, "I want a divorce. This is not the life I planned! You would be better off without me."

He was right. It was not the life we planned. Yet we had faced and overcome each challenge that had come at us. Why stop now? What was he really talking about? My hero—my six-foot three hero—seemed like a tiny boy. He talked about his childhood in Alabama. The overt racism and segregated life he lived were unimaginable to me.

"They paid me to leave Birmingham. Don't you know that if a black man gets educated, he's seen as dangerous? I'm going to get my education!"

I didn't know what it was like to live in the segregated South, but I did know New England. O.D. had learned a lot about the North—had even tried skiing—and he maneuvered our boat around Portland harbor like a native Yankee sailor. One night when we were driving off to a social event, I noticed the aurora. The northern lights were shimmering on the horizon. When I was a child, I had seen them in pastel colors but this night in Maine they were white ripples, dancing across the sky.

"Oh look, the aurora!" My excitement met with silence. It was as if he had not heard me.

"What? What is that?" he demanded. "aurora? No! No, it's the end." He turned the car around and brought us home. He was convinced that it was a sign of "the end." *The end of—the earth?* I couldn't get him to make any sense. Facts, my experience, nothing I said reassured him. I felt defeated and alone. How could nature terrify this big, courageous guy? I convinced him to go to counseling.

I made friends with an elderly Jewish neighbor who lived in the next apartment. We met in the laundry room and had great, long, talk sessions. She was a widow and had a unique outlook on both life and death. We talked about love, life, death and husbands. She was a loving, trusting friend who had no faith in banks. She gave me instructions on what I should do if she were found dead.

"If the apartment should ever burn, go in the refrigerator and take the mayonnaise jar. . . ." We confided in each other. Mrs. Goldberg would often hear me lamenting about this paradoxical man, my husband.

Work-mates at the Medical Center were also very friendly. They shared their struggles; partners dying, illness, forced moves to accommodate care of failing parents. It seemed that my challenged marriage was not so bad after all. O.D.'s friends at the Training School in Pownal drew him into their circle. Our parents and siblings came up to visit and we entertained them. Ted and his friends had a great time cruising around with O.D. in the boat.

His commute from Portland to Pownal wore the old car down and we bought a new one. Money was always tight. Orchestrating transportation, fetching the sitter before I went to work, getting me back home at midnight and meeting O.D.'s increasing work commitments became more and more challenging and a new source of contention. It cost more for me to work than the aggravation it caused was worth. After a fiery debate about whose responsibility it was to pick up the babysitter, I decided to quit working. O.D. rented an apartment in Yarmouth, nearer his workplace. Neither of us had consulted the other; verbal discussions or explosions did not resolve any issues. When O.D. came home from work and decided not to sit at the table for six o'clock dinner, I became furious. The meal was ready and the baby and I sat waiting for him.

"I want to watch the news. Bring my dinner in here." It was a simple request, not a demand, but my reaction was in keeping with my fury. With all the strength my seething body could harness, I sent him his silverware airborne express. They flew just inches away from his face and clattered against the wall of the living room. In calm silence, he joined us. My behavior frightened me and again I sought counsel. In our sessions, I focused on our disagreements and different ways of handling money.

"Why do you have a joint checking account?" the Reverend Goodwin asked. "You complain about working to cover rubber checks. Why complain? You *do* have other choices here."

It had never occurred to me to close our account. The priest concluded that money might seem like the problem but, in truth, I had not yet begun to face the real issues—I could not imagine what those issues might be.

I had not seen the new place O.D. had rented and had to convince him that we should not move in the night. While he began to move furniture, I negotiated with the Office Manager at Forest Park to release us from our lease without financial penalty. Once we relocated to Yarmouth, the tension seemed to ease. It was an interesting old house with a great deal of charm. From the long, closed-in porch, I could see men building ships on the water's edge. I set up house and got to know our new landlady. Lee was a younger mother with twin eight year old daughters. Our Laurie was more than a year old, learning to talk and enjoyed the twins who were gentle and patient with her. Her first sentence came tumbling out when we were driving over Tookey's bridge in Portland. The B & M bean factory flanked the ocean to our right, and then we could see the entire harbor.

"See the boat!" She was beaming and pointing her tiny finger at a small, sun-bleached boat riding in the waves like a bathtub toy. This picture-puzzle view and the aroma of baking beans always made this ride enjoyable. I was gloriously happy. Our baby was growing up; she had quickly given up diapers, was very steady on her feet and took pride in choosing her clothes from her own dresser. O.D. had painted Disney characters on the wardrobe panel door and drawers. She and her daddy were great buddies, sharing a loud, romping humor that often escaped me.

The nearby lakes were very warm in summer so I took Laurie and the twins to Little Sebago Lake. Laurie had been paddling in water before she could walk. The ocean water would make my toes curl and cramp, but we took quick swims there too. The mist off the water would roll in each afternoon, making my clothes damp if I didn't hurry to get them in. I would often iron them dry but only fussed with dresses and shirts. Keeping house was a pleasure.

Our doctor-prescribed birth control failed again so I went back to work part-time on weekends just to get ahead. We did not need a sitter because I only worked the night shift. After my three-month checkup, the obstetrician blithely announced,

"You're not pregnant."

Preposterous. I knew I was paying him for prenatal care and this was *not* my first visit! It was a long time before I could speak. My mind flooded with memories and the mysteries of my first pregnancy.

It had been a complete surprise and, during those eight months, I was told that my anemia was a sign of Sickle Cell disease; that I might have a bihornate uterus or twins and was asked if I ate clay or starch. I experienced a high leak of amniotic fluid from a tear in the membrane. How they knew from a vaginal exam, I couldn't figure, but it may have resulted from the car accident we had, when my cousin Richard bailed us out of a hostile police station outside of D.C., late in that first pregnancy. I did not eat clay or starch. I did not have Sickle Cell anemia, a bihornate uterus, or twins. I had a pedunculated fibroid tumor that grew as rapidly as the pregnancy and had flattened itself on the outer wall of my uterus at full term.

Laguno hair is usually not visible on newborns. It swooshes away with the amniotic fluid at delivery. I had a dry birth and after twenty-four hours the hairy little being with side-burns and eyebrows that covered her forehead became my first beautiful baby girl. My nursing

156

textbooks and my clinical experience did not cover any of these weird things.

"What do you mean, not pregnant?" My voice was an echo of my feelings.

"There's only one explanation. All the signs of pregnancy are gone. You have a missed abortion. There's little we can do now, your uterus is highly vascular, and it's not safe to consider a D. & C. We'll just have to wait. Most women spontaneously abort." He rambled on.

"The baby is dead?" Nothing else he said made sense.

"Oh, there's no doubt. You could carry for a few days or a few months. Keep taking your prenatal vitamin; your hemoglobin is very low. If you start cramping or bleeding, give me a call and we'll proceed from there. Are you OK?"

I was numb when I left the office. In some fashion, I told my husband. He did not seem puzzled or curious. His projects kept him away from home all day and some nights and he was busy helping a work-mate through some personal problems.

I was *not* OK. I carried a dead baby for five months.

Laurie and I had come home from a bus trip to Portland when the first cramps came. I called O.D. at work but he was not in the office and no one could tell me when he would return. When the bleeding started, I called the work-mate whom he was helping with the personal problems. I allowed my suspicion of an illicit affair to surface. She did not know where he was, but noted the insecurity and worry in my voice. Without being asked, she arrived at my door, gathered the baby and me into her car and drove us to the hospital in

Portland.

"How much are you bleeding?" someone asked in the admission room. I had grabbed a Turkish towel to protect the car seat and showed them. It was saturated. There was no more conversation, just a flurry of activity.

"We have to be sure there are no retained secundines. Did you use the bathroom? What have you had to eat? You must go to surgery and we must type and cross you for a transfusion." They wanted all the answers but paid little attention to my questions.

"Yes, we saw the fetus; it's mummified. No, we can't tell if it's a boy or a girl. There's a great deal of maceration." My questions were finally answered but my refusal to allow a blood transfusion became a major issue. In my nursing experience blood transfusion errors occurred far too frequently, resulting in very serious consequences. No blood, no errors! I was on my way to surgery when they reached my physician and informed him of my refusal of a transfusion. He reluctantly honored my wishes. I held my position the three days I was in the hospital and, on the day of discharge, my blood levels had improved.

It was a long while before my hopefulness and exuberance returned. O.D.'s job offered sabbatical leaves, with half-salary for two years. We figured we could sustain ourselves especially if I worked part-time, so he applied. He became driven and agitated and it showed in the long hours he kept at work and in the aggressive way he acted out in our bed at night. Our newest birth control prescription failed.

My landlady Lee and I talked about the mysteries of birth and death. She understood my strange elation upon discovering I was pregnant again. The quiet sadness that lurked in the recesses of my mind lifted. I had not realized how real the loss had been until Lee and I talked and cried together. O.D.'s reaction to the news was flat, unemotional. He seemed consumed with his work and hopes of recognition for his efforts at the Pownal School.

"Aren't you a little pleased?" I ventured. "*I* was surprised. Aren't you even a little surprised?" My questions did not draw him out and his feelings remained unknown to me. I talked with Lee and my nurse friends. My life was manageable. O.D. and I did not continue with our counselors as traveling to Portland was time-consuming and sharing the car only happened on weekends when I worked. O.D.'s therapist had violated confidentiality by speaking to his peers about our participation in counseling; the therapist's peers were O.D.'s colleagues. Our friends became our confidantes.

It was a balmy summer day and I had been in town with the baby. Lee—who had become my closest friend—greeted me in the doorway with a barrage of questions.

"Shirley, what's going on? I was talking to O.D. and he says you're not pregnant, and that you're moving!"

O.D. was in the driveway, ignoring both of us. A U-Haul trailer was hitched to the back of our car and several boys from the school were helping him to lash down our household goods.

"What happened? What are you doing?" His answers came slowly.

"I resigned today. The rest of our stuff is in storage and I'm bringing you to your mother's. I just have to bring the boys back. Come on, we're ready to go."

Laurie's dresser, my kitchen canisters, and all our clothing were jumbled together in the open U-Haul. Mute and frozen, I clung to Lee; trying to say thank you, trying to say good-bye, trying to comfort my toddler and calm the quickening infant in my womb. I felt like a wooden image of myself. On the long ride to Massachusetts, I heard isolated details.

"This is the third and last time they're going to turn me down! I *trained* the guy they gave the sabbatical to. I have seniority over all the psychologists in my department. I'm the only one who has had works published. How dare they turn me down!" O.D. grumbled and muttered. He was not talking to me.

"It's just because I want to go to Howard. The University of Maine at Orono may be near, but it's not *my* school. Howard has already accepted me and that's where I am going!"

There was no real conversation or understanding between us from that day forward. That was more than forty years ago.

I wrote an apologetic letter of resignation to the Director of Nurses at Maine Medical Center. She was a good ally and attended Trinity Episcopal Parish near our first apartment in Portland. My temporary stay at my mother's house was extended unexpectedly. Worcester City Hospital hired me without hesitation and, with help from my family, no-cost childcare was worked out. O.D. found part-time jobs in Washington, DC, and was living in the back of a funeral parlor, but was unable to pay the storage company. My family helped me salvage some of my household goods. Sears Roebuck repossessed my rugs and the washing machine although I had already paid for them.

"On a revolving account, ma'am, we take anything we can resell. Are you sure you don't know where the boat is?"

O.D. and I wrote to each other. He was looking for a place for us to live. He planned to find me a job and, after the baby came, he could put Laurie into a boarding school and his relatives would look after the newborn. Some of my thoughts found their way to paper, but much of my agonizing stayed battling in my brain and haunted my sleeping hours.

"What does he mean, a live-in school for Laurie? She's a baby herself-only two and a half! I can find my own damned job, thank you, and I can take care of my own baby."

We remained at odds. My mother had never had love in her heart for O.D. Whenever he was around my family, his anxiety tripped him into unforgettable faux pas such as his forgetting to drive Audrey and me to the church on her wedding day. The bride and I tucked ourselves into her car and drove to the church, arriving just a wee bit late. It had been healing for me to see how truly confident and capable he could be when my family came to visit us in Maine. He did not panic in their presence when we were in our own home.

My mother felt justified in her judgment of my husband when we arrived unannounced at 12 Ellen Street. She commented on how much my young one reminded her of O.D. It made her furious that my little girl wept herself to sleep at night, calling for her daddy. Laurie could not be comforted and sometimes she would sob until she vomited. My mother did not keep her comments to herself and insisted that evil made the child gag and vomit.

"You can't take care of two babies! It will be a blessing if that baby in you died."

I had a repeated nightmare where I would see a yellow, mummified infant inside me. In desperation, I got help from the Worcester Child Guidance Clinic. They helped Laurie through her grief with play therapy and *my* therapist helped me regain the ability to sleep without nightmares and without grinding my teeth. Autumn slid by and, in midwinter the new baby, Mary Elizabeth, arrived. I called her Marybeth. She was a beautiful girl who amazed the nursery staff with her tears. Most newborns do not shed big, shiny tears moments after birth.

O.D. drove up to see us when the baby was eleven days old. It was the Washington's Birthday holiday weekend, and he found a way to get himself to Worcester. I did not realize or appreciate all that he had to overcome in order to see us. My mother greeted him with a verbal attack.

"You need to take care of your wife and children! She can't work—she's on welfare. You haven't sent a penny to help! What kind of man are you? I run an elevator and I can hardly feed *myself*. You'd better get over this school stuff and meet your responsibilities. Just who do you think you are?" Stored venom spewed up from her toes and flew at the man who represented every man she had ever loved and lost. He matched her tirade.

"You're her mother! Why haven't *you* been helping out?"

It got worse. His loud voice filled the house and filled my brain with panic and sorrow. They were both raging, defensive, out of control and beyond reason. I had packed some of our belongings in anticipation of leaving with him. Finding work for myself in Washington, D.C. did not daunt me. Taking care of my newborn and my toddler would certainly challenge me, but I was more than ready to leave my mother's house—it was no longer my home. O.D.'s behavior towards my mother alarmed me. She ordered him out of her house and now I had doubts—his verbal attack made me wonder who he really was. I handed him our belongings. They were mostly wedding gifts, things not needed in my mother's house. It helped me to begin my emotional exit from my her home. I silently decided it would be up to me to figure the whole mess out. I was sure I was not going to leave with him that February day so I put all my attention on surviving.

I can do this. General Relief is all welfare can offer until I establish residency. O.D. can find something. In a few months, I'll be back to work. If I do part time, Ma can help with the girls. I'll have them ready for bed.

Neither my mind nor my body rested for the next year. The Youth Guidance Center became my anchor and my sanity. Laurie went to a private nursery school that supported the play therapy she received at the Center. She was no longer the focus of her grandmother's resentment and my mother's attachment to the baby filled the emptiness she had harbored since her daughters had left the nest. With my family's help, my daughters were thriving. I hoped my newly created family would be reunited with every passing month. We needed our own place. The conditions that would allow our going to D.C. became more rigid, and our marriage collapsed onto a shaky ledge. O.D. never returned to

163

Worcester. We exchanged letters, but neither one of us seemed able to understand the other's situation. My mother lived in fear that O.D. would drive up any day and take the children.

"That's the way he'll get you back! Don't be so naïve. He hasn't sent you enough money to feed a cat! He wants you to keep working yourself to death while he gets his damned degree. You've got no sense at all—*that's* all he ever wanted from you. Why do you think he ran off after these babies came?"

She would go into tirades about O.D.'s not sending enough money—education was a luxury to her. I filed for Separate Support to establish myself as Custodial Parent. This would prevent the children from being taken from Massachusetts and the courts would require the father to pay child support. This action calmed my mother but did not generate any financial help as O.D. moved to a new state each time I petitioned for support—Virginia, Maryland, Alabama and the District of Columbia. A knock on the door and papers served by a Sheriff ended the stalemate after another year had passed by. O.D. was suing me for divorce.

***

Mother had a green thumb. Given a broken stem or a leaf, she could grow a plant. African violets and rose begonias were her specialties. Each riser of the steps leading to the bedroom held well-tended, vigorous houseplants. She used narrow glass cinderblocks, lining them up like a miniature wall to close in the open steps so that the plants would form a living balustrade for the living room space below.

"Do you know what your baby did? She watered my plants with Prell Shampoo! It's taken me all afternoon to rinse off the roots and re-pot my plants—and I'm not through yet!"

There remained enough space on the broad lower risers to put small things that could rest there until she carried them upstairs: things like combs, hairbrushes, a small pile of folded washcloths or the sprinkle/spray-top plastic bottle she used to hold shampoo. I could picture my little one imitating her grandmother, loving-ly sprinkling each glass pot with a bit of liquid. I want-ed to laugh and I would have if I had not heard the angry frustration in her voice. Marybeth could do almost no wrong, but this was a major offense. We moved.

The Great Brook Valley Housing Project had a wait-ing list. The Garden section of this large project was very attractive in the early 1960's. Flower beds huddled by the back doors and clotheslines were enclosed behind cedar wood fencing in the center of the large common courtyard. The row houses, with four duplex apartments, had one-story units at each end reserved for the elderly.

"But, Mr. Jasper, why must I still wait if you have vacant apartments? I've been on the waiting list for a long while."

"We have to keep the units balanced. That's how we do it."

"Balanced?" I suspected that he meant racially bal-anced.

"Each unit has elderly married couples, moderate income and subsidized income tenants. Since you are a single parent, you will be in the unit on Constitution Avenue. There's only one other single parent in that unit. We maintain a good social balance."

It sounded illegal to me. The escalating civil rights movement had made me sensitive to social engineering schemes. However, we were accepted and moved in.

Our Great Brook Valley days were very special. The Project was a true community. The Sullivans, our next-door neighbors had a big family and adding one more for lunch was never a problem. Pat Sullivan made grilled peanut butter and jelly sandwiches that Laurie described as scrumptious. She started first grade at her new school. Parents shared childcare and my neighbors and their children were welcome in my house. We went to orchards, picked bushels of peaches, shared them and made peach marmalade. My neighbor's children were part of the cooking crew. There were special programs for the children and Laurie took dance lessons. We became a productive, active family of three.

My rent was forty dollars a month. Because I was on General Relief, I had a social worker who was required to make inspection-type visits.

"What kind of toothpaste do you use?" (Mrs. Pervia's questions confounded me.) "We have to ask these questions. I know you want to get back to work but for now, I will record that your mother is helping you get your car. You will have to surrender your license plates if I don't. If you start to work now, it will be January before they raise your rent. Then you can save your money and move out of here."

She offered sound advice and I followed it. I began part-time work and my little one went to The Happy Day Care Child Center near my mother's house. Having my own home made life hopeful again. In January of 1965, my rent went up to four hundred dollars a month so I found an affordable apartment right in my old neighborhood, on Sunderland Road. I had spotted it on my ride to Marybeth's nursery school. Laurie was in third grade and Marybeth started kindergarten that year. They both attended Roosevelt, my old grammar school. I had come full circle.

480 Sunderland Road became another special place. We had three rooms on the second floor. In the Project, the girls had had their own room and I set up the new house so they shared the one bedroom and I slept on the folding couch in the living-room. It was cozy. Sunlight bathed the kitchen and brightness filled each room. The girls had their first pets: a cat who had several litters and gerbils that reproduced so prolifically that we were able to sell the new generations back to the pet store! We grew and became enlightened together. I learned a great deal from them.

The girls were playing outdoors as evening fell around us. I felt chilly sitting on the back steps watching their game.

"Come, girls; put on your sweaters!"

"Mommy, why is it when *you're* cold, we have to put sweaters on?" My young one's tone was serious, not a bit sassy. For a moment, I was simply speechless.

"Aren't you cold?" I had never considered the possibility that they could not be cold.

"No, mom, we're sweatin'!" She gave me that information and ran off to finish the game. They grew up like Alaskan blossoms in twenty-four-hour sunlight. I taught them to cook and clean and keep house with youthful expertise—which means that I never discovered the dried peas behind the refrigerator, artfully tossed there seasons before we moved, and our oven became so encrusted that my landlady was horrified. Laurie broke her ankle swinging under the handrail and jumping off the back stairs. Her sister and their neighborhood classmates cut her boot off, iced her leg and left her at home on the couch to wait for me to come home from work. They made an agreement that she would call me at work if the pain got worse but she did not call because she did not want to upset me. They became experienced problem-solvers. We had a good sense of each other and ourselves as individuals and were also close to family and friends. As a family, we discussed current events, said prayers at night and functioned as a team. National and local politics gave us a great deal to talk about; the media was no longer censored and family- friendly. The six o'clock news contained raw data: assassinations, war scenes, police brutality and explicit social insanity.

When Old Mr. Sanda—our neighbor across the street—had to go into a nursing home, we talked about how wonderful it would be to rent his house. I was perplexed when his daughter called me the same week. Somehow she had information that I was interested in renting her father's house.

"Tell her 'yes,' Mom!" My daughters were waving excitedly as they figured out who had called. "We wrote a note and put it in Mr. Sanda's mailbox. We signed your name. You're not mad, are you?"

I was speechless, then gathered my wits as Mr. Sanda's daughter continued to talk. "We have to liquidate all Dad's assets in order to pay for his care. We'd like to sell the house. Would you want to buy it?"

The price was reasonable and after a few sleepless nights, calls to the bank, a lawyer and a quick call to my father when the Sandas told me they had another buyer, I bought the house. I still live in it. The Sandas promised to empty the house, but after I bought the stove and refrigerator they never returned. His silverware matched mine. The master bedroom dresser and matching headboard became Laurie's bedroom set, then it was my nephew's and now it is mine. My ambitious plans to renovate the bathroom faded quickly, allowing me to continue to enjoy the claw-foot bathtub. New windows, new wiring—but the old house is much the same today as it was when we moved in years ago.

"Shirley, I just love your house. It's sooooo Victorian!" A friend noted the conglomeration of furniture that now filled my house. With the remnants of Mr. Sanda's tools and odd leftovers, there have been a few more things added. For example: piano rolls and old records from my grandmother's house when it was torn down, and a few things from my Aunt Carrie's place on the Cape; bric-a-brac and costume jewelry from my Aunts and photographs covering every available open space. I asked another friend what she thought a Victorian house looked like. "Victorian? Well, a Victorian house is cluttered, full of all kinds of ornamentation and stuff." The description fits. It is my fantasy to hire a person who will help me organize, categorize and preserve the wonderful collection of "stuff" that I have accumulated in my house over these many years, just as writing this memoir has allowed me to organize the clutter in my rich, colorful life.

**Daughters in Wagon with Cousins,
Dottie & Betsy**

CHAPTER 25

Henry Wiesbauer

Rob, Father McKenzie's son, led me back into the Episcopal Church. We had attended Classical High School together in 1946. His search for unchurched Episcopalians opened an opportunity for him to become an evangelist and initiated my long relationship with his family and an even longer relationship with St. Matthews. My children grew up in the parish and two of their children were christened there.

I have no memory of the Roman Catholic Church my father had belonged to in Cambridge. He and his siblings attended parochial school there and my sister was christened in Sacred Heart Catholic Church in Cambridge. My recollections of my church experiences at All Saints Episcopal Church are sharp and poignant and I undoubtedly shared a particular memory when talking to Rob.

Father McKenzie loved his parishioners and like a kindly parent, defended unchristian acts by exclaiming, "People have good hearts, but sometimes their heads are full of feathers!" He frequently attempted to excuse the behavior of some of the older parishioners, many of whom were of English heritage. Most of the "old" families in the parish were born in England and came to Worcester to work in the M. J. Whittall Mills.

They had strong ties to St. Mary's, their parish in Kidderminster, England. The Whittall mansion was across the street from St. Matthews and the mill owner built houses for the imported workers. One such woman believed she was giving us a compliment as her face beamed in admiration at the sight of my six nieces and nephews.

"Oh my" she gushed, "they are beautiful—and so clean!"

I was offended and felt the comment was insulting. That kind of unaware racism infuriates me because the person often defends the mistake and remains blind to the reality of racism! My sister adopted Father McKenzie's attitude towards unaware, unkind behavior and simply replied, "Soap's cheap" and continued on her way.

There have been many changes in St. Matthews over the years. Father McKenzie answered a call to Caribou, Maine. He died there while at the altar preparing for Mass. Before a new priest came to St. Matthews, we had a series of interim priests. During the 1960s, one of those interim priests, Father Henry Wiesbauer, served our parish. He never failed to inspire me to think critically and to scrutinize my behavior as a Christian. Henry Wiesbauer was a vigorous, passionate priest who delivered zestful sermons. His model of Christianity was genuine and for me, personally instructive.

One of his first sermons made me wonder what kind of Christian I was and later, his challenge led me to act far outside of my usual, passive, ceremonial church role.

"On my first parish assignment," Father Henry explained, "I introduced myself by putting on a big, old topcoat. I arrived early, before Mass and sat on the front steps of the church. I had a brown bag with a bottle in it and splashed a bit of liquid on my coat. Parishioner after parishioner arrived, walked around me, and never so much as looked into my eyes. I thought about doing that here at St. Matthews and wondered if any one here would have dared to even say hello. What would you have done?"

He continued, describing how he was shunned, and how challenging it is to put one's faith into practice. I feared I would have been one of those who walked by, or worse yet, one who asked him to get off the steps and go to a proper shelter. As I listened, I prayed I would have—at least—looked at him. His sermons often haunted me.

Father Wiesbauer's Easter sermon nearly moved me out of my seat. He presented his sermons and homilies as if they were conversations.

It was the resurrection story and he was describing the women who first arrived at Jesus' empty tomb. He paused and asked a rhetorical question:

"What do you suppose the women said?"

He paused again, comfortable with the silence. My mind wandered, searching for an appropriate answer. In a loud, hysterical tone that echoed into the rafters, he wailed—

"Whooo stole the body-y-y?"

The sharp anguish in his voice made me gasp and riveted my attention. An old familiar story had come alive as Father Henry told it. Most sermons, before Father Henry came, had either put me to sleep or stimulated my imagination, causing my mind and my attention to go elsewhere. One way I tried to look attentive

173

was counting the times one of our priests repeated the phrase, *"as it were."* Father Henry was never boring.

Life in the 1960s was anything but boring: passion and violence dominated the news media. Father Wiesbauer ended one of his sermons by informing the parish about a Civil Rights march happening in nearby Springfield. He had made tentative arrangements for transportation so that St. Matthews' parishioners could join the march and he asked for a show of hands of those who would be joining him. The church pews were full that day, but only one man raised his hand. It was my brother-in-law, Ernie Brown. Father Henry stood at the pulpit in silence for what seemed a long while. My sister Audrey vigorously pulled Ernie's hand down.

"You've got six children! It's not safe. You are not going!"

With stunned restraint, Father Wiesbauer restated his intention to march and invited anyone who might have second thoughts to ride with him in his car. I left church bewildered and numb with my fellow parishioners. Perhaps we *all* had second thoughts. I felt as if I had let Ernie down and Father Henry too. I looked at my two young ones: Laurie was in preschool and Marybeth was still a lap baby. I needed to act for *them*! I couldn't stay shocked and frozen at other people's inability to act or my own fears of violence. Thinking that I had hesitated too long to ride with Father Wiesbauer, I asked my mother to look after my little one and took my firstborn with me to Springfield.

There were hundreds of people in the streets as police directed me to a car lot and Marshals organized people into squads. I never saw Father Henry. What my little one and I saw were crowds: young, old, black, white and the religious in habits—a throbbing sea of humanity. It was terrifying. National Guardsmen stood with rifles poised on every rooftop. We walked for about an hour and then the crowd began to disperse, swarming in every direction. We hurried into the car lot and, trembling and teary, I locked my car doors and hurried home. As panicky as I felt and as terrified as I was, I knew that it was the right thing for me to have done. Taking my daughter was my attempt to take a visible stand, to witness in a manner beyond words. Father Henry Wiesbauer led by example and he modeled being true to one's faith, and I treasure his memory and the gifts he shared with us at St. Matts.

CHAPTER 26

Working I

MUNICIPAL WORK

I continued to earn money in my younger years. At Worcester City Hospital School of Nursing in 1949 to 1952, a stipend was paid to students. Pay was issued at City Hall: cash—thirty dollars—in a small, oblong, tan envelope. The stipend was ninety dollars a month and the School withdrew sixty dollars for maintenance. My sister and I pooled our cash, sharing fifteen dollars each and giving the other thirty to our mother. We bought stockings and minimal necessities, managing quite well.

After graduation and a bout with the mental health system, earning a living was never a problem. I enjoyed my nursing assignments: Winslow Surgery, women's medical surgical and orthopedics at Worcester City Hospital, obstetrics at Georgetown, DC, and float nurse at the Maine Medical Center in Portland. When I returned to Massachusetts, I often did private duty along with part-time medical-surgical at City Hospital. A nursing shortage in the nineteen-sixties brought new challenges and competitive salaries and the Worcester State Hospital offered the highest pay scale. Unionization, management disputes and overtime issues changed the climate in general hospitals. Patient care was no longer the primary focus of nursing management. Private duty allowed me to continue giving quality care at the bedside but eventually I went to work at the Worcester State Hospital. I did staff nursing there, specialty Day Care nursing and finally, supervisory nursing and staff development.

Working in a team in the Staff Development Department was most enjoyable. Our Director of Nurses, Kathleen Coutou, made it possible for the nurses to earn college credits at the Saint Augustan Institute which was the evening division of Assumption College, an all-male Catholic college that originated as a preparatory school. The curriculum at the prep school was presented in French and administered by priests. I took courses part-time for years and eventually earned my bachelor's and master's degrees in education.

Entertainers, the poor and people of color had struggled with addictive drugs for years, but the nineteen seventies heralded the spread of drug culture to middle and upper class young people. Public Health officials, school boards and government agencies became alarmed, passing laws requiring drug education in schools. Drug prevention, first aid, nutrition and venereal disease education were mandated in Massachusetts. Staff development, teaching supervision, Assumption College, Kathleen Coutou and fate combined to change my career path to public education. School departments were recruiting registered nurses with education degrees to teach Health and Safety in secondary schools. Physical education teachers with overloaded schedules—one or two teachers were servicing the total population—had been pressed into fitting health classes into their packed day. They ran to classroom spaces in their gym attire; showed films such as *Reefer Madness*, then ran back to do their real work in the gymnasium. Money was allocated in order to support the new law and Mrs. Coutou encouraged me to accept an offer to teach at Worcester East Middle School. One of *her* unrealized dreams had been to be an educator and she encouraged me to seize the opportunity or live a life of wondering or regret. She helped me barter for a better salary and allowed me to work two weeks of night duty in order to submit a professional resignation while attending the new-teacher orientation required by the school board.

***

WORCESTER PUBLIC SCHOOLS

After thirty years of nursing, I became a classroom teacher. One of the lingering adjustments I had had to make while nursing was to cope with bad weather. New England snow and ice-storms require nurses to rise earlier, scrape, shovel and get on duty on time. If a storm struck while I was on duty, I remained at work until a person on the oncoming shift got there. If the snow was too deep to drive, he or she was driven to work by snow crews or the police.

"Snow day, snow day, Ma!"

My daughters would hear me rattling around in the gray morning hours, bundling up to go shovel.

"Ma. Go back to bed!"

It took a couple of winters before I became as excit-

178

ed as the girls when storms were predicted. School cancellations were a novel and happy circumstance. I found classroom teaching physically and emotionally more exhausting than nursing, but the snow days, summers off and vacations more than compensated for the challenges. I was also on the same schedule as the girls and that made teaching a pleasure.

I enjoyed the eighth grade students. They were in the between-age. One day they would be itchy and dry as hay, the next day soft, delicate, and fresh as newly sprouted grass. They were passionate, sophisticated and testy one moment, then childish, sweet and endearing in the next. Their energy and curiosity left me drained at the end of the day, but their candor and honesty made teaching Health and Safety a joy. Funding came with the mandate for teaching health and my budget allowed me to buy good textbooks, magazines and state-of-the-art mannequins for teaching rescue breathing and cardiopulmonary resuscitation—CPR. Some students in my class earned instructor status and taught CPR in their scout troops. My subject was classified in the curriculum as "Enrichment." That meant I taught every eighth grade student.

A Black Social Studies teacher, Barbara Spence, mentored me in Black History and enlightened all the students. We learned to stand for the Black National Anthem and Martin Luther King was honored and celebrated. When Black students were singled out and forbidden to wear head-wraps, Barbara alerted me and we devised a subtle protest—we *both* wore African head-wraps and students wearing tasteful head adornments were no longer harassed. My youngest daughter learned African dance and performed on stage at school. Black awareness came into my life like a lost relative returning home.

My career goal now was to teach health teachers, so when a position was posted in the Staff Development Department, I bid for it and was hired. It felt good to be part of a team again. Our innovative ideas were supported and I initiated a pilot drug-prevention program for elementary grades. Due to the civil rights acts of the nineteen sixties, programs had been developed to train and hire more teachers of color. The Urban Education Department at the University of Massachusetts at Amherst graduated increasing numbers of Black and Hispanic teachers, curriculum specialists and researchers.

The 1980s brought fiscal austerity. Many programs were interrupted but our department, Staff Development, was eliminated! A taxation cap called Proposition Two and a Half, that had been supported by the majority of Massachusetts voters caused massive municipal layoffs. At Worcester East Middle School, there were two black educators. Staff development had had none before I came to be one of them. White flight now changed the complexion of Worcester's schools. Role models for inner city children became an urgent topic of educational conversation. Sugarcane field-workers from Puerto Rico came to Worcester in search of a better life. Boat people from Haiti and from many countries in South East Asia, filled the chairs of local students who had fled public schools and now crowded the private and parochial system. The teacher's union included Affirmative Action language to reflect the changing face of education. The plan supported the recruitment of qualified minorities and created percentage formulas, which ensured that a proportionate number of the new minority hires would be retained in case of layoffs. They lied. When layoffs became a reality, nearly every minority educator received a pink layoff slip.

Betrayed and angry, I got together with a group of minority educators and filed a grievance with my local union, the Educational Association of Worcester which is a branch of the Massachusetts Teacher's Union. Some felt unsafe signing it and waited to see if they might be recalled in the fall, thinking they could jeopardize any chance of being rehired. It was clear that September would show a shortage. The cutbacks were drastic. Police and firefighters sought legal counsel and so did we. Some of their contracts contained language designed specifically to prevent the last hired from being the first fired. My local union representative would not submit or support the grievance. The Affirmative Action Officer was in an administrative position and so could not submit a union grievance. The personnel Director could not help, so I went to Boston to the state union association. They would not support me nor provide counsel because they were opposed to the use of affirmative action language in a layoff situation.

Because my department had been dissolved, I was reassigned to Middle School Health Education. The department was new and small. My coworkers found it difficult to empathize with my protest: if I was retained, it meant that one of my white coworkers with more seniority would be laid off. A small group of us minority educators sought our own legal council. We had a ratified contract with protective language. A Worcester firm advised us of the expenses we would accrue and referred us to a group in Boston: the Lawyers' Committee for Civil Rights. They were a subcommittee of a prestigious law firm that offered pro bono services to select cases. My social studies colleague at Worcester East Middle School had received her layoff notice. Barbara's support and perseverance motivated our small group of protesters. We had to raise funds in order to initiate our case. *Pro Bono* status did not cover all the costs our case required so I sold my bed at our yard sale and went door-to-door in my neighborhood, soliciting donations. The committee took our case and we did research, ran errands and served summonses— I served our local union president at Logan Airport. We sued the union, the School Committee and the City Council. They all negotiated and ratified our contract. When the case went to court, I was on the stand for several days. Opposition lawyers attempted to minimize and belittle the injustice of the contract violation.

"Why did *you* file a grievance? *You* didn't lose your job! Why are *you* involved in this litigation?"

"Because I'm Black!"

Their tirade finally stopped. Our attorneys worked tirelessly and supported us well. We were all asked to leave the courtroom while the deliberations concluded. Our small group huddled outside the closed door. One of the two teachers in our group who was named Mary, began to hum softly. Barbara, Ann, Earlena, Debbie, the other Mary and I listened and those who knew the words began to sing softly:

"He didn't bring us this far to leave us . . . ."

Bystanders in the hall held silent while we lifted our voices in prayer. We *won* an injunction that interrupted the layoffs and prevented the firing of *every* minority in the *first* year of the Tax Proposition, but the union held their position.

"We negotiated that affirmative action clause in good faith. We did not anticipate there would be layoffs. The intent of affirmative action was for recruitment. We have no choice with jobs at stake—we have to revert to the oldest law of the land, seniority!"

They were unabashed when they admitted they used the affirmative action language as a device to recruit with no concern about retention. The case continued for several years, went to arbitration, and ultimately became legally moot when the Supreme Court in Washington ruled in favor of seniority over affirmative action.

For the next three years, I continued to work for Worcester Public Schools. In June, I'd receive my layoff notice, and in September, a recall notice. The second year, Health was eliminated from the middle school curriculum and I was assigned to North High School to teach at the ninth grade level. There were few supplies, a shortage of classroom space and a short supply of old, defaced textbooks. The students were disenchanted. The following year, Health was eliminated at the freshman level.

CHAPTER 27

Arrest Racism!

There were times when racism flared and although my mother had invested a great deal of time instructing me on how to behave when confronted with racism, I had no thoughts about the next generation. When I was a young girl, trying to figure out the irrational responses my color seemed to evoke, I had not planned to be a mother—I was going to be an aviatrix. Parenthood never crossed my mind and I had already made the decision not to resemble my mother in any way. I did become the mother of two little girls, by choice and by chance. My little Marybeth and Laurie had many encounters with racism.

It was the '60s when my young ones went off to school. It was no longer politically correct to call oneself colored. The civil rights movement and the image-makers chose Black or African-American. The older generation still thought of itself as colored, (militants were black) and politicians used whichever adjective got the vote. Media folk, as well as others were left wondering just *what* to call people who were not white.

My little girls did not understand why some classmates called them "nigger."

"He kicks the back of our seat and calls us names all the way home! Why does he do that, mama?" they complained and questioned. The old *"sticks and stones may break your bones, but names will never hurt you,"* was not an adequate solution. That same kid came to the fence near our house and began taunting and name-calling. I grabbed him by the scruff of his neck and dragged him two houses down to his back door. When his mother answered the doorbell, she showed no surprise. She listened placidly while I registered my complaint and served notice that this unacceptable behavior would not be tolerated. He never came to the yard again, but he took every chance to sit behind them on the bus and would kick the back of their seats, quietly calling them names all the way home. The girls no longer reported his ugly behavior. He was not the only name-caller, but his family had lived in the neighborhood for a couple of generations. I had grown up in this neighborhood and my Grandfather had taught neighborhood boys how to raise homing pigeons. This kid's dad was one of those boys and that made it seem worse.

"Let *him* look the fool. He'll grow tired after a while, especially if he doesn't get a rise out of you." It was not the kind of advice Dorothy had given me. They took my advice but the infernal kid never stopped. We talked together about Martin Luther King's nonviolent approach but the news kept irrational, racist, violent scenes in our faces, night after night. Police officers, Sheriffs and Governors spewed hate, shot tear gas, hosed and harassed people who looked just like my little girls and myself. They killed children, students and white sympathizers. Passivity was not in my heart, but I feared for my daughter's lives and instructed them to follow Martin's method of protest.

Marybeth, my younger girl, was the first to experience the violence and hatred of racism firsthand. She loved music and dancing and other young people of color. There were no children of color in her neighborhood except her first cousins, but gathering in dance halls were groups of Hispanic- and African-Americans confirming their identities, taking pride in who they were and trying to figure out ways to support each other in the face of overt, deadly racism. The dance halls attracted shady characters, dopers—and cops.

An unfamiliar young voice on the telephone tried to tell me not to worry:

"Don't get upset—there's nothing to worry about now. I'm a friend of your daughter's and she asked me to call. It *will* be past her curfew, but she'll be home soon."

The pause allowed me to bristle. I wondered, *What kind of lame excuse is this going to be? A curfew is a curfew and these are not the times for leniency.* I knew I had to say what I meant and mean what I would say. The girls knew that too. I was already thinking about suitable punishment, some loss of privilege, when the somber tone of the young voice caught my full attention.

"I ran and got away when the cops came. My parents have already gone down to bail Mary out. The cops grabbed every kid on the corner. They raided The VIP Lounge; shut it down right after they opened up tonight. They threw everybody in the Paddy-wagon. Mary's got a bump on her head . . . they didn't hit her, just shoved her and she got bumped against the door—but she's OK. She told me to call you so you won't worry. She missed her ride home—we all ran for it!"

Whatever else the young caller was trying to say was drowned out by my panicked voice.

"*What? What did you say? Who are you?* What were you children doing at the VIP? Who else was there?" I did not wait for answers. My voice filled my ears and my thundering heart made the telephone useless. I could not hear a thing. Fear and rage commanded my tongue.

"What is your name? How much is the bail? What was the charge?" My voice had raised an octave and my brain could not grasp the sequence of events.

"*Please,* please Mrs. Carter, don't get so upset. She's OK, and she'll be home, real soon!"

I could not be reassured. My older daughter heard the panic in my voice and chimed in with another barrage of unanswerable questions. The call ended. By the clock, it was not long before the friend's parent drove Mary home. No one could tell me the cost of the bail—only repeated reassurance came from my child and these "friends."

I went to court to hear the charges and stood with my daughter before the judge.

"Mary Carter and Company." The clerk called just one name but there were at least a half a dozen young people of color, mostly boys. The children were silent and somber. There were no other parents present. My daughter and I had talked a great deal before we came to the courthouse.

"Mom, I did exactly what you always said we should do. The cops were *really* mad . . ." This child had stood with her friends. She would not run, but made certain that one who did run would get word to a trusted adult. The young boys had resisted; had tried to reason with the officers, explaining that they were just watching.

Tempers flared, but Mary silenced her friends and advised them to behave as she had been instructed.

"Be polite. Don't give them any reason to treat you badly." As she spoke, the police turned their force on her and pushed her willowy body through a door not tall enough to accommodate an erect person. When the officers demanded names and ages, she remained the calm spokesperson, just as she had instructed her friends. The lump on my child's head was still noticeable. Her contact lenses had been dislodged and lost when they jammed her into the police wagon. It was all too real, too ugly and too fresh in my mind. I fought to keep down my rage.

"According to officers . . . you are charged with obstructing a sidewalk at such and such street on the evening of such and such . . ."

It was over quickly. My thirteen-year-old child was completely composed.

"Young lady, you stay out of trouble until you are sixteen."

The judge spoke personally in a paternalistic tone. He wanted her to know that the charges would be sealed, but they never left my mind. I spoke with one of the boy's parents long after the court date:

"Are you still upset about that? Oh come on now, you know they just wanted to shut the place down. The kids were gawking. You know how cops are . . ."

No, I never saw it as an ordinary event. Children had been charged with obstructing a sidewalk. They were shoved, jailed, bailed—and saddled with police records that would only be sealed if they managed to stay out of harm's way for the next three or four years. The VIP Lounge sign still haunts the vacant storefront on the corner of Chandler Street and Murray Avenue: a sad reminder of a place once filled with music, laughter and young people dancing with danger while trying to find each other.

Laurie, older, (now called Laura), in Junior High, had her racial agony imposed on her by black class-mates who called her names for not "lining up" with black students when racial tensions flared at school. Teachers and school administrators attempted to defuse the rumble by evacuating the dining hall. Blacks were to go out one doorway and whites the other. Laura left with her grammar school friends, who all happened to be white. She withstood the name-calling and stood fast with her friends, but never rejected the students of color. Latinas embraced her. Blacks often shunned her and Laura ended up protecting her younger cousin Betsy from physical intimidation by black girls.

CHAPTER 28

The Learning Tree
A poem of pain at 1:55 AM

Her tree is so big and tall

—but she's not small.

It scares me to watch her climb.

Is it the time?

I can't sense the joy,

the excitement,

nor appreciate the view.

Is it the tree?

Is it me, or is it **you,**

that **scares** me so?

Shirley in Uniform

CHAPTER 29

Working II

UNIVERSITY OF MASSACHUSETTS MEDICAL CENTER

After repeated school layoffs, I went back to full time nursing on Five West, a Pediatric Mental Health (Psychiatric) Unit. We admitted newborn babies and children up to age sixteen. An infant diagnosed with *Failure to Thrive* could be admitted to this small, unlocked unit. It was challenging duty. Often we had a mock family mix of a few very young ones with grade school children and one or more teenagers. The professional staff worked diligently to diagnose and refer, while creating a safe, structured, learning environment that met the needs of disturbed children. The children dramatized the chaos in their troubled families. We called them *symptom bearers*: pointing out the malfunction in their homes. Stability, routines and loving attention often led a child from a silent, dark or bizarre demeanor into recognizable relief, hopefulness and even jubilance. It was satisfying, demanding, labor-intensive work. I was recalled in September to teach upperclassmen at North High School. When I went back to teaching in the fall, I continued to practice nursing on weekends.

The students were not interested in Nutrition, had already made decisions about their choice of drugs and were frighteningly depressed, disillusioned and disinterested. One out of three worked hard for their grades, were involved in every school opportunity open to them and succeeded very well in my health classes. Some could not remain awake or attentive for more than a few minutes during the class period while others were absent in mind or body. I began to hate my job. I worried about the freshman students I had come to know and respect who were now smoking. Not just cigarettes, which were allowed out on the school grounds, but they were also smoking marijuana. They smoked pot in the bathrooms and outside my window in clear view. I expressed my concern to the principal.

"Oh, Shirley, they'll be gone before I get down there. At least they're out of the building." I was horrified at his lack of concern and spoke to the students directly.

"Jheeze, Mrs. Carter, don't worry. We were only tokin.' Look, we'll find a new place, honest. *Pah-leeze*, don't get so upset."

I never stopped feeling upset, but they did find a new place out of my sight.

When I worked weekends on the Pediatric unit, I was Shirley, the nurse—the woman who played around-the-world basketball, crab soccer; swam with them in summer and went sledding in winter. I never told the children I was also a teacher. Many of them had traumatic school histories and had been medicated at school to control their frustration. To my surprise, one of my teen-aged patients was assigned to my health class. One look at me and she ran out of the room.

"You're spying on me! Why are you doing this to me?

Who sent you here?"

She ran to the office crying, demanding that I leave the building and leave her alone. "Stop her from following me!"

The office called her social worker to come and return her to the unit. When my class was dismissed, I went to the office hoping that she would still be there. The school secretary saved the day. She knew both of us very well and helped the student understand that her "Shirley" was also Mrs. Carter the Health teacher and that I had indeed been teaching there for a couple of years.

North High School made me depressed. I tried everything I could imagine to make the course interesting, active and challenging: guests, films, peer surveys, and finally I sent the one-in-three achievers to teach in the elementary schools. They had audiovisual materials and worksheets from the Lung Association, the Heart Association and the American Cancer Association. My plan required meetings with Quadrant Managers, parents, Principals, and I relied on family members for transportation—both the student's family members and mine! It was exhausting, so in 1985 I went on Sabbatical leave and finished my Doctoral degree.

I continued to do nursing on weekends. The Pediatric Mental Health Unit had closed because it did not show a profit, so I worked Friday nights on the Adult Mental Health Unit.

When I returned to work at the schools, health education was only being taught at the eleventh grade and North High School no longer needed two health educators. I was assigned an itinerant position teaching at the fifth and sixth grade level in a quadrant cluster of schools. Traveling teachers had five or six schools they rotated to during the week. There were Spanish-only groups that necessitated interpreters, and hearing-impaired groups who required signers. I taught hundreds of sparkling, exuberant children. My car broke down. I misplaced my belongings and lived a management nightmare for the year shuttling between all those schools. It seemed to me that this was no way to do a truly good job, so I took an unpaid leave and went back to nursing. A coworker on the adult mental health unit was surprised and pleased that I was taking a break from teaching. She was attending Springfield College, earning a degree in Community Health. The College was scheduled to undergo an accrediting process and was desperately in need of professors who had classroom experience teaching health. She informed the college and vigorously urged me to talk with the acting department head. My doctoral degree had enhanced my salary at Worcester Public Schools, and my nursing paid equally well, but the starting salary for an Assistant Professor was abysmal! It took several conversations, an interview, and a day-long visit before an acceptable salary was negotiated. To maintain my level of income, I worked at my nursing job on the adult mental health unit each Friday night.

***

CHEAP LUNCH

Assistant Professor of Health Education was an interesting, challenging job. I worked with a brilliant colleague and met outstanding young adults. There was excitement layered with variety and topped with surprise. My schedule changed every semester, as well as my course responsibilities. My office space changed annually. My colleague, Ken Romer and I revamped the entire curriculum, bringing it up to and above certification standards. Nothing was easy, but the satisfaction factor energized both of us. The highlight of those two and a half years was Freshman Camp. Most faculty members groaned at the mention of this unique program but Ken and I enjoyed it immensely. It was a wilderness experience, required by the Health Education Department and several others. Faculty members assisted and supervised freshman students while they learned to pitch tents, cook and bake using camp stoves and earth ovens, start fires without matches, negotiate outdoor showers, work in cooperative teams and—by week's end—strike camp leaving no sign that humans had been present. We pitched our tents and stayed with the students throughout the entire experience. It was like watching caterpillars spin into their cocoons; at first shrinking away from the challenges then, at week's end after tears, trials and tribulations, emerging as wildly excited, beautiful butterflies, capable of flying off to anywhere they might choose.

The administration was in a state of upheaval. They were vigorously campaigning to establish two tracks of professors: tenured and contracted. Ken and I were slated for the new untenured track, which the older faculty members did not support. Newer members, like Ken and me, were made to feel like pawns or scabs, willing to upset years of tradition in exchange for money. We had already signed contracts and were being asked to accept the certainty of never being tenured. After two years the controversy intensified and looked more like an inflammatory scheme, a done deal with no true option.

I commuted, driving or busing two hours each day. There were many heated evening faculty meetings that I did not attend. Ken, who lived nearby, did attend and often spoke up. The health education department had gained a new Department Head, replacing the temporary Physical Education Umbrella Department Head. The new department head, did not discuss the controversial school politics, but found curious ways to alter the newly accredited department. Most department heads were male and this historically all male "jock" school exhibited sexism in peculiar ways: female faculty had to walk long distances to rest rooms and evidently, female department heads were not taken seriously. Ours acted like she was on a vendetta.

We could no longer get services from the PE department, yet we had no secretary. One shared work-study student became our "clerk." Requesting vans for student transportation, once a simple procedure, became complex. While awaiting new approvals, trips had to be delayed. Our office spaces were "relocated" without notice. Performance Evaluations had to be written, yet the new department head had *no time* to come to our classes. She was *uncertain* about my performance because student evaluations were *mixed*. I had hundreds of student and taught several courses. Mixed evaluation? Of course they were mixed! Frustration became the norm.

The dining hall had a big-screen television and Ken and I watched the space ship Challenger burst into a ball of fire and disintegrate before our eyes. It was an omen. The Health Department began to fall asunder. Ken's contract was not renewed yet I was offered a raise, which required me to sign another contract.

Did they expect me to instruct the entire department? Ken was open and honest and initiated most of the innovative ideas that made our department interesting and attractive to students. If his excellence and dedication were not valued, what would be my fate? Fall guy? How could administration be so arbitrary? What part are they expecting me to play in this political fiasco?

Ken and I had long lunchtime discussions and seriously considered our options. We made an interesting discovery while standing in line in the cafeteria. Ordinarily, I carried my lunch. I would have my brown bag and supplement it with soup or a beverage. My lunch was cheap. Ken habitually ordered a hamburger, French fries and a beverage. This day, I ordered the same. My routines were disrupted, my mind preoccupied and I had not bothered to make lunch. I paid with a five-dollar bill and got a handful of change. Ken paid the same and received no change. It must have happened at other occasions, but neither of us had noticed. I *always* got change.

"Wait a minute! How come you charged me more than Dr. Carter?"

The embarrassed student cashier gave a strange explanation.

"Uh—well, Dr. Romer, faculty have to pay the full price, but-uh-students don't have to."

"Students? *Students!* You thought Dr. Carter was a *student?*"

"Ya, Ya, I thought so. I used to think . . . . Oh, I just

forgot."

The student knew me from class, but had been cashiering before we met. *All* the cashiers had *assumed!* The only full-time professor of color, I had been sold cheap lunches for two-and-a-half years. When the college did not renew Ken's contract, I resigned.

Teaching has benefits that are unheard of in the nursing profession. I enjoyed having summers off as well as every holiday. Working with young people—generally healthy young people—is a refreshing change for a career nurse who has seen end-stage illness in every age group. Mastering multiple challenges at Springfield College gave me a sense of prowess. I went to the Personnel office at Worcester Public Schools, feeling that I would give the itinerant schedule another try.

"We don't have any openings in your department, and you no longer have any seniority." The Personnel Director smiled wryly as he gave me the information. "You'll have to resign—we no longer have a position for you."

The sardonic grin froze and curious, almost worried wrinkles gathered around his questioning eyes, when I informed him that I had no intention of resigning. He had been party to the suit the Minority Educators successfully initiated during the Tax Rollback years. My plan was simple—legal recourse was not on my mind. I strolled across the hall to the benefits office. With thirty years of municipal service and having passed the age of fifty-five, I retired from Worcester Public Schools.

***

A NEW KIND OF NURSING

The field of nursing offered variety. I continued working part-time on the Mental Health Unit and tried my hand at Home Health Care. It resembled the private duty I had done in the past, but now the patient took the lead and the family was integrated into the care plan. It seemed like a positive direction for the nursing care of tomorrow. A national chain of Home Care Providers bought out the first local agency I worked for and everything grew. They hired more staff, offered more training and focused their services into narrower, specialty areas. My previous assignments had included elder home care, temporary staff replacement in drug rehabilitation facilities and at the State Hospital, administering medications in schools, and occasional pediatric care. I replaced the nurse instructor at our local Job Corps site, teaching a nursing assistant training program. Some Home Health Care assignments lasted a day, others—like the Job Corps—lasted for weeks. Pediatric cases were the most challenging. The new management increased the number of ventilator-dependent patients along with intensive pediatric cases. It became increasingly nerve-wracking. I was a girl Friday for a young quadriplegic. Once a week for one semester, I accompanied this young man to his school, pushing his motorized chair when it stalled, carrying his computer and wand, along with his suctioning and emergency ventilating equipment plus his books! I learned many new skills and took more night-duty cases.

***

CUL-DE-SAC

Nightshift pay is often the best and the physical demand is less intense. Most of my cases involved machinery. One complex case involved a woman who lived out in the county. She had multiple feeding lines, drainage catheters and a ventilator. My assigned shifts gave the regular nurse two nights off. When I arrived at eleven o'clock, her husband would go to work. Two nights at a time was all the anxiety I could comfortably handle. I drove to the house one night and discovered that I had made my turn a street too soon. Both streets were horseshoe-shaped cul-de-sacs with lovely big homes designed by the same developer. The house numbers were identical, but there were small architectural variations that made me aware of my mistake as I climbed the front steps. I quickly returned to my car and drove to the twin cul-de-sac. Before I could pull in to the curb, two police cruisers blocked my car.

"Where are you going?" The officer asked with genuine curiosity.

"I'm reporting for duty at this house. What's the matter?"

They requested to see my license and identification. I was wearing my agency badge and showed them my credentials.

"I have to relieve Mr. 'Blank' so he can get to work. Is there a problem?"

They were taking their time, scrutinizing each item.

"Who do you work for?" Patiently, I gave my agency's name, but they did not move their cruisers until after they called the agency, waited for the answering service to page the on-call night supervisor and talked with her. I was late for my shift and steaming mad. The patient's husband thought it was the funniest explanation for lateness that he had ever heard. He was still laughing as he left the house, late for work. I was left trying to imagine what the family one street away said to the police as they saw me approach their steps and wondering why the officers found it so difficult to process the information I gave them. Racism is a crazy-maker!

CHAPTER 30

The Gift

I hiked myself up to peer over the side of the gondola as we glided over the lake. There it was, reflected below—a perfect image of the giant balloon. Its bright colors fixed the majestic view in my mind. This awesome experience moved so slowly that the eyes could linger to grasp the enormous image. This time of my life was like the balloon: colorful, full and serene. I was gliding; I didn't feel the wind—I floated on it. There was time to absorb the benign serenity of nature above and below, a time to reflect on life. The pilot, two other passengers (a father and son), my daughter Laura and I moved across the countryside like a summer cloud. Occasionally a dragon breath of the propane roared a jet stream of fire that lifted us higher above the treetops. Silence reigned.

My children were grown. My firstborn, Laurie—who stood beside me this day—left home for college at seventeen. Marybeth left at sixteen, completing her last year of high school simultaneously with her first year of college. They had established their own adventurous lives: graduated, traveled and worked in Europe. They experienced their own triumphs, trials and tribulations. As my daughters had done, I too had earned advanced degrees and my sister, Audrey, had given me this gift—a balloon ride for two—to celebrate my recent graduation. The poverty and isolation of my youth was far behind me as I stood under the mantle of bright silk colors that was holding us aloft. The vibrant combination of colors resembled my many friends, my extended family, my colleagues, work-mates and allies that had hovered around me in times of need.

The skilled pilot who guided us this day expressed his concern.

"The wind speed is carrying us further than I expected. The tracer truck can't keep up with us so I'm looking for a good clearing where he can spot us." His voice exuded assurance; his face reflected wisdom as he smiled and pointed out a meadow to us. The only way a hot air balloon can return to earth is to crash-land.

"When we hit ground you all know what to do." His trust in us was amazing. He'd shown us before we went aloft how to collapse the huge balloon lest the winds fill it and drag us into peril. In my life, I had encountered peril, had struggled to collapse the inflated circumstances that had threatened me. The most pervasive of all the ill winds was racism; it always boded evil, dragging me down and wreaking havoc across the world.

We hit the meadow, tumbled out and made the pilot proud. We packed in our gear, took off the helmets and waited for the truck to retrieve us. As promised, we celebrated our adventure with a champagne tailgate party.

In my personal life, I had chosen God as my pilot. The ups and downs, the unexpected, the fiery dragons, tossed me about, but as the colorful balloon had done, I would return to solid ground. I trusted God and believed in the goodness of people and had even come to love and respect my father. He had given me the gift of life and, as adults, we had struggled to know each other. An absent father when I was a child, he made a tremendous effort to be an attentive grandfather to my girls. When he was dying in St. Elizabeth's Hospital, his final words stayed with me. Lapsing in and out of consciousness, he opened his eyes, looked and smiled as he advised,

"Drink all the wine . . . savor it all." And I did.

CHAPTER 31

Men

There remains one puzzle in life that I will perhaps always have to work on—and try to comprehend. It's men: the other half of the human race. Loving them has been a struggle, but understanding them seems easier than when I was young. I can now see how they try to hide their fears and often feel badly about themselves. Badly about not meeting the social expectations: not measuring up or succeeding according to some elusive social definition.

Some expectations of society include men being expendable: valued for their work yet the first to be sent to war, expected to remain behind on a sinking ship, and necessary collateral casualties in war or when con-structing tunnels, or canals, digging in mines, or accomplishing any physical challenge. Even men I have come to know well and love dearly, mystify me. Oscar, the man I married, was proud to be in a special Army unit where men were dropped by parachute behind enemy lines with special assignments—and *no* plan or expectation to ever rejoin their unit! Then there's my youngest grandson, Jascha, who can initiate a conver-sation about wolves that will leave me sad and enraged.

I romanced a fellow for thirty seven years only to discover we could see each other clearly, but couldn't look in the same direction and build a life together. That's my old friend, Lee. My daughters were in kindergarten and third grade respectively when mutual friends introduced me to Lee. Our relationship is still prized yet unresolved.

Other men like my dear friend Peter who can magically fix a persnickety light bulb I couldn't make work, can be so stern with others that I cannot hide my surprise. To me, Peter is sure, clear thinking and direct. He cares about me and shows it without hesitation.

Peter and I met in the 1970's when we were both teaching Health Education in Worcester Public Schools. We both love young people and when we taught, were committed to making a difference in our schools. Schools sometimes fail to appreciate the wonderful humanness, natural joy, beauty and intelligence that children embody. Their zest, along with their curiosity, energy and passion, required creative classroom strategies in order to present useful lessons in the arbitrary time slots that schools allotted to health teachers. When I taught, I used to contract with students for their grades. It was fun; it saved precious time and made them partners in the learning process. Not "giving" grades removed the biased adult interpretation of work done by worried young humans trying to please rather than to learn and enjoy the process. I had four hundred and fifty report cards to grade but did not have to do averages nor make any arbitrary judgments. I'd spell it all out:

"This is what you need to do to earn an A. To earn a B, do this . . . ." and so on down to a failing grade. It was a win-win proposal—the only way to fail in my health education class was not to show up. I saved the drafts of the various contracts, student signatures and their comments about using contracts. They held precious memories and were a lifesaver when I had my daughter in class. Her classmates speculated that she would get an A.

"Hey, Mair, what'd you contract for? An A, huh?"

"No way," she told them. "She'd work the pants off me to earn an A. I'm getting a B!"

Years after Peter moved out of state and still taught, he made an appointment with me to explore the possibility of using contracts to grade his science students. I was no longer teaching middle school, but he remembered what a joy contracts were for me. We were deep in discussion when my friend Lee came by. Lee and I were dating, but never committed to being life partners or were even in an exclusive relationship.

"We're working on school stuff," I explained.

"OK, I'll wait 'til you're through." Lee had come into the kitchen where we were still engrossed in adapting the contracts to a science curriculum. Briefcases, papers, grade books and contracts covered the kitchen table. Lee paced about the room.

"How long have you been here, Peter?" This was the first in a series of inquiries and interruptions. They seemed innocent to me, but were unappreciated intrusions to Peter. The men's voices became hostile. The room felt small. Diplomacy was my first defense when the ugly tones rose and danced between them.

"We won't be much longer." I offered a suggestion: "Why don't you come back in a bit?"

"Go into the living room and let us finish up!" Peter's tone was not diplomatic. He chose not to mask reality as *he* saw and felt it. Lee went into the living room but chose not to be silent. His feelings about Peter always had an edge of suspicion or fear. Lee could not see how a man and woman could love one another without being sexual. Peter and I are dear friends, not lovers.

"Jeez, you've been at this for hours!" Lee quipped from the next room.

"Look! I made an appointment." Peter yelled into the living room. "Shirl, did you know he was coming over?"

"Hey, Lee just drops by—it's no big deal." I wanted them to tone down, to be kind to each other.

Peter made his declaration firmly. He spoke slowly to Lee, "This is my time. You're annoying. Just go! Come back later."

"What! Are you trying to kick me out of *her* house? Who do you think you are?" Lee moved back into the kitchen. His dark face was a tight mask of defiance, wide-eyed, lip curled.

I held my breath and began to shrink in the presence of these beloved males. I was small again and silent; frozen in an old memory of Dorothy and Herbert.

"Just get out of here!" Peter's voice commanded.

Lee looked at me for assurance, or for some confirmation. "Do you want me to leave? This is *your* house!" My tongue was paralyzed. He left, slamming the door behind him. Weeks passed before he came calling again. Peter and I finished the meeting, then reflected for a short time on what had happened. My casual 'taken-for-granted' relationship to Lee needed definition. Lee's feelings of possession were out of place. Peter advised me to sort out my feelings and clarify the relationship. I love Peter and never fear that he will be confused about his feelings of affection or of mine. This is a precious gift and to me. My love relationship with

Oscar ended so suddenly and painfully, I fear showing any emotion around most men.

***

On a more recent visit, Peter had come during the winter holidays and we had a well-orchestrated plan to enjoy a bit of time together before I went to work. I was working the night shift. I delayed going to sleep in the evening, which was my usual routine. Peter and his friend Lilley, who lived in Vermont, were supposed to attend a social event near Worcester. Since Lilley had friends and relatives in Worcester, she was going to visit with them after dropping Peter at my house. She chose not to get out of the car even though it would be a short visit and she was welcome. I had to leave for work in just a couple of hours, yet it was a lovely opportunity.

"Lilley doesn't pay attention to time. We made plans. She agreed!"

Lilley failed to return and pick Peter up so they could continue on together to their holiday event. His terse statement was matter-of-fact: "Of course I'm annoyed. I'm a man of my word!" He telephoned his friend and was prepared to accept nothing less than the terms agreed upon. She was to come at once. Lilley made some explanation he was able to accept—once I offered to drive him to the house where they were to spend the rest of the evening. I would go from there to work. *Why was he so rigid? Why didn't she even enter my house? Was she jealous?*

It all worked out, but his annoyed tone made me shiver. It reminded me of that time when Peter and I made plans to work together on the student project he was exploring. Peter and Lee had clashed many years before, yet Peter's tone with his friend Lilley put me into the same frozen state. I agreed to drive him because it felt as if I would end up in the middle of a feud. It had been such a good holiday visit, brief, but well thought-out and precious to me. The sharp edge stayed in his voice until all the wrinkles were smoothed out of his plan. Then, in just three hours, we squeezed in all the important happenings in our lives that had occurred since our last visit.

That same winter day before he left, Peter noticed my dark living-room light. I had taken it apart in an attempt to fix it when a tall guest had bumped into it, causing it to spark and blow out. It didn't work when I put in a new bulb. Peter proceeded to check the wires and we explored it together. We tried another bulb—it worked! My whole life brightens when this man shares time with me, yet fear lurks in the recesses of my mind when his voice is raised. Men's voices seem to hold violence on a short leash. It seems to be a part of the culture of men.

I've finally come to grips with the fact that men are different, not just in the way they are designed, but in the way they think and the way they deal with the world. Men are direct and often act superior and sound arrogant. I can already hear it in my youngest grandson's voice. He has Peter's male determination and expects things to go his way.

***

JASCHA AND THE WOLVES

Sober concern haunted Jascha's handsome seven-year old face.

"Grandma, do you know what an alpha is?"

"Well, to me alpha means first, or the Greek number one. What does it mean to you?"

I was cautious not to say too much as it was a pregnant kind of question. We walked silently from my car towards his house. I'd pick him up at his car pool or school bus drop off and stay with him for a couple of hours until his mom came home from work. He loves his house and all its things that are there just for him. It is truly his place, safe, loving—meeting all of his needs.

"Well, Grandma, the alpha is the top wolf. He rules. Do you know what the 'betta' is?"

"That means second, right?" I pronounced it more like I had heard it in church, *bayta* (beta). I wondered how the Greek word alpha and wolves got to weigh so heavily on this young one.

"Yup. He's next! The betta gets to challenge the alpha. You see the alpha gets the food first, and then the betta gets it next. Grandma, do you know what the *scapegoat* means?"

"That's the one who gets picked on. Sometimes people pick someone to scapegoat just because they're small or different. It's never fair, just a mean way to treat other people when folks don't feel good about themselves. They try to imagine they are more by making someone feel less." The long answer was more than Jascha had patience to listen to. He had a story to tell. He interrupted.

"Well, I was the betta at school today. I like being the betta. That means I get to challenge!"

We were already in the house, starting to build with geometric blocks and setting up his alphabet train track. He kept silent, still pensive as we built skyscrapers and peopled the city with army figures and aliens. I ventured to draw him out.

"So who was the alpha at school?"

"Oh, Danny and Bobby."

Both names were familiar, but one name caught my attention. Bobby was a name-caller and a bully. I had challenged his warped behavior several times when the children got off the school bus together. He would get loud and taunt the smaller children.

"Why do you have to do what she says? Who is she, anyway? My mother doesn't care what I say. You're a weenie, just a weenie, and you don't even know what a weenie is! Ha ha, Jascha is a weenie!" He'd use foul language, sang dirty ditties and try to get Jascha to sing them too.

"Julie read us a story about wolves. The scapegoat gets to watch out for the children." Jascha rolled away from the blocks, made gun sounds and moved the figures in the toy town we'd built. I waited.

"I like being Bobbie's betta. It's fun to get knocked down."

"Who was the scapegoat?" I asked gently.

"Oh. Mary."

I had met her at Jascha's last birthday party. Mary was overtly competitive and robust and her brothers were her mentors. It was difficult to imagine her playing the role of the scapegoat willingly.

"You might know," I lamented. "Sometimes a girl

213

will take a lowly spot like that just to be included in the game. It really isn't fair. But sometimes that's the way it is, even in the business world."

"Well," Jascha chimed in, "There's one good thing about being the scapegoat. Once the alphas and the bettas are through fighting, the scapegoat can just eat what's left! No one bothers the scapegoat."

I wasn't sure if this was a real game or a conversation that the children had had after their teacher read the story. I worried that pushing each other down might get a bit out of hand.

"Do Danny and Bobby really push each other?"

"Oh, when I'm the betta, they push me, but I just get up. It doesn't hurt." He sighed, and did not speak for a long time. I respected his silence.

"You know, Grandma . . . I was the scapegoat." His voice was quiet and sad. My heart began to fill with rage. The scapegoat! A hint of suspicion had risen when he first began to describe the play-yard acting out of the story. Inside my head, I seethed. How dare those bastards play those crappy games at school! Where the *hell* was Miss Julie when those privileged white male oppressors pulled their alpha crap! What kind of a Goddamned world is this that perpetuates this animal dominance crap on human beings? My rage ebbed and sadness blanketed the playroom. I spoke first.

"It's hard being the scapegoat. It is *never* fair or correct to make someone feel bad, even as a game."

Jascha recited how the scapegoat got to be the hero in Julie's story by watching out for the young wolf pups.

"*Pachew, pachew, pachew!*" Jascha's gun sounds startled me back to his world of play.

214

"Grandma, can you build another skyscraper? Mine keeps falling down."

"Sure, let's build it together. We need a firm, solid foundation. The rug is too bumpy. Here—let's use this cardboard, then leave more spaces between them, then we'll have more blocks to build it higher."

Jascha is learning about the testosterone-driven world of males. He is destined to be an alpha and knows what he wants. Danny and Bobby have another agenda. They have noticed the way their teachers behave around Jascha's mother. They beckon to her but do not open the door. They smile too broadly. Miss Julie asks that Jascha's mom wait before she visits the classroom. She wants the children to settle in first. But *Bobbie*'s mother was immediately invited to do a project with the class.

I am living in the twenty-first century. Parents and teachers are still expected to identify children by race. The October report is done so that schools can qualify for moneys allocated by the federal government according to race categories. Some families leave questions unanswered or chose *other* when race identity is requested. These are families like Jascha's. I have a tremendous responsibility to help the next generation succeed in a world where white privilege, capitalism, colonialism and imperialism still rule. I can show them how to build skyscrapers that house dreams and goals. Their foundations are already strong. All they need is space to stand tall and soar to whatever heights they chose. My grandchildren are *other*. Their mothers are colored, of course.

CHAPTER 32

Threes

"They come in threes, you know. I wonder who will be next?"

This is one of the ways that old women talk about death, but the number three did play an interesting role in my life. There were three Rickards girls. The middle sister, Dorothy, was my mother. She was born in 1903. Dorothy had three pregnancies while married to my father. I was her middle pregnancy. Nine months later, the third infant died shortly after birth. Within the next three years my father had left my mother and proceeded to marry his third wife, Hazel.

Our house on Ellen Street remained home for the three of us; mother, Audrey and me until my sister and I went to nurses' training. We moved into Thayer Hall and lived there for three years. Married at age twenty-five, I became a wife and mother for three years, lived in three states and experienced three pregnancies. Three was like a repeated theme. My husband left "temporarily" more than forty three years ago. I made a home for my two daughters and we remained a family of three until they moved into college dormitories. There are three years difference in their ages. I currently have three very special grandchildren, Ariane, Liam and Jascha, who confirm that the number three is enveloping, enclosing and though odd, is a familiar, comfortable numeral in my life.

CHAPTER 33

Spririt Pool

We come and return to the spirit pool, a reservoir of quickening; where rays of joy transcend . . . to light a spark, evoke a levitation, surge a cluster of intelligent cells housed in a living thing and prompt it . . . to create, expand and become a part of this temporal existence until the cycle turns and we come soaring home!

I am an incarnate ray from the spirit pool and see the splendor of the clouds, filtering beams and generating splendid earthly pools of ice and mist aided by the power of the daystar. The flash of the aurora, the splendid arches of color in the rainbow. . . the prisms and twinkles forever reminding me of the highway home, back to the eternal . . . the spirit pool.

Adieu

Index of Photographs

Cover (left to right)
Audrey E. Barrow Brown & Shirley F. Barrow Carter
Circa 1936

#1 - Page 13 - Sisters in Winter Coates
 L-R Audrey Brown & Shirley Carter

#2 - Page 19 - Newly Built Roosevelt School
Roosevelt Grammar School 10006 Grafton Street,
Worcester, MA 01604
Circa 1920

#3 - Page 21 - Gram and Grampa Rickards
Laura F. Washington Rickards   (b.9-21-1875 d. 7-3-
1962)
Elias Edward Francis Rickards   (b.9-27-1867 d. 11-1-
1937)

#4 - Page 23 - Dorothy Lee Rickards: teenager
Dorothy Lee Rickards Perkins Barrow (b.10-17-1903 d.
9-2-1977)

#5 - Page 29 - Aunt Carrie Pocknet
Caroline E. Pocknet (b. 8-8-1869 d. 8-2-1941)

#6 - Page 33 - Twins in Halloween Costumes
Cover Photo: Audrey & Shirley

#7 - Page 37 - Dorothy & Elsie Rickards and Doll
Dorothy Lee Rickards Perkins Barrow and sister
Elsie Viola Rickards Hampton (b. 7-22-1900 d. 2-12-
1954)
Circa 1906

#8 - Page 44 - Gram Rickards on Mark Hayes' Wall
Laura Frances Washington Rickards
Circa 1940

#9 - Page 46 - Mother with Hampton Kids
Dorothy L. Rickards with nephew, Heywood Edward
(Brother) & niece, Evelyn Lauraine (Rainy) Hampton
Circa 1925

#10 - Page 52 - Herbert Aaron Barrow & Dorothy Lee
Rickards Perkins Barrow
Circa 1930

#11 - Page 104 - Miss Scully
Kathryn C. Scully, RN: Supervisor of Private Service
Instructor of Professional Adjustments, 1952

#12 - Page 139 - The Other Mrs. Barrow with Her
Children & Shirley
(L) Emma Moore Barrow, (R) Shirley F. Barrow, front
Anita Marie Barrow, center Willinda Moore Barrow,
front Herbert Aaron Barrow, Jr.

#13 - Page 140 - O.D. and Shirley with dog, Worcester
Oscar Dillihan Carter & wife Shirley F. Barrow Carter
Dog from the Worcester pound

#14 - Page 146 - Audrey's Wedding Party with Shirley as Matron of Honor: Wedding of Ernest Cornelius Brown and Audrey Elizabeth Barrow
June 1957 @ St. Matthews Church, Worcester, MA
L-R: Dorothy Wellwood Peden, Lois Marie Perkins Cato, Geraldine Peterson, Shirley Barrow Carter, Bride & Groom, best man Alan Roots, Oscar Dillihan Carter, Daniel Robert Hampton, David Wellwood.

#15 - Page 148 - Shirley with Baby Daughters
Shirley F. B. Carter with daughter (center) Laura Frances and baby, Mary Elizabeth
Circa 1960

#16 - Page 170 - Daughters in Wagon with Cousins
L-R: Elizabeth Ann Brown, Mary Elizabeth Carter, Dorothy Ellen Brown, and Laura Frances Carter
Circa 1962

#17 - Page 191 - Shirley in Uniform
Shirley F. Barrow, RN 1952

Back Cover:
Shirley & Audrey in Argentina @ Iguazú Falls
Caratas del Iguazú
May 2003

CPSIA information can be obtained
at www.ICGtesting.com
Printed in the USA
LVHW012335271019
635506LV00017B/749/P

9 781597 130271